January 1988
To Bill Quick —

Should you enjoy these
messages half as much as we
all appreciate yours, then I have
proffered a worthy gift...

With my highest respect,
Bill McCue

CLEARING
THE
GROUND

It is ambition enough to be employed
as an under-laborer in clearing the ground
a little, and removing some of the rubbish
that lies in the way to knowledge.

— JOHN LOCKE

Books by Sydney J. Harris

CLEARING THE GROUND

Sydney J. Harris

1 9 8 6

HOUGHTON MIFFLIN COMPANY BOSTON

Library of Congress Cataloging-in-Publication Data
Harris, Sydney J.
Clearing the ground.
Essays from his column in the Chicago Sun-Times.
Contents: Of the social animal — Of the life of
the spirit — Of the mind and passions — [etc.]
I. Title.
PS3515.A762C5   1986   814'.54   86-15275
ISBN 0-395-42645-6

CONTENTS

PART I

OF THE
SOCIAL ANIMAL

It All Depends on Who Says It

YOU CAN SAY the most unflattering things about your own group to members of your own group, and they will customarily not take offense. Often, they will laugh with you about the perceived defects or excesses of the group. But try saying some of these same things about people outside your group, and you are very likely to be castigated, condemned, or even boycotted and picketed as an "anti."

I witnessed an example of this not long ago, when I attended an all-black dramatic presentation, which was a coarse burlesque of black habits and manners in a northern American city. The audience, which was mostly black, seemed to enjoy this caricature of a certain type of lifestyle. Yet I am sure that if the same presentation had been put on by a white company, to largely white audiences, it would promptly have been denounced as a cheap travesty, and just as promptly labeled "racist," for its selectively slanted portrayal of the black community.

This is a nearly universal trait: We resent it when outsiders say about us what we may sometimes privately say about ourselves — because we feel that they are saying it out of ignorant malice, while our observations are tempered with sympathy and a degree of understanding. The Irish feel free to mock some of their own cultural traits; so do the Jews or the Hispanics — but no one else may dare to make the same sardonic comment without being accused of being a snob or a bigot, and being called to apologize for such a slander.

Americans are in much the same position when they visit Europe or other parts of the globe. At home, we may criticize many of our attitudes and insensitivities toward the rest of the world. But we cannot help bristling when we hear foreigners criticizing American commercialism, our overbearing manner, or our provincial prejudices.

We spring to the defense of our country's ways much more quickly and ardently than we are inclined to do within our own borders. Somehow we assume as a right what in outsiders we regard as an impertinence or an insult, a flagrant display of anti-Americanism.

A great part of getting along with other people consists in the recognition and acceptance of this double standard that is implicitly held by all groups. It is the source and direction from which the criticism comes that is resisted and rebuffed more than the comment itself. I can say about me what you are not permitted to, and the louder you keep saying it, the more I will deny that there is any truth in what you say.

Insanity among individuals is much rarer than it is among groups, factions, sects, and even nations — but then it is no longer considered to be insanity.

∎

Chief executive officers who insist that their object in administering is "to be respected, not to be liked," are not respected either, if their attitude is unlikable; what they take for "respect" is only fear and resentment, which eventually cripple the morale of an organization.

The Man Makes Us Believe the Oath

LONG AGO, an ancient Greek playwright wrote the memorable line "It is not the oath that makes us believe the man, but the man that makes us believe the oath."

I recalled this adage when I was leading a college seminar that examined and compared the constitutions of the United States and the U.S.S.R.

The Soviet Constitution is a noble document, but it is only a piece of paper, and hardly anyone outside the Comintern takes it seriously. The U.S. Constitution is much more restrictive, but it is devoutly respected and followed by the branches and agencies of our government.

It is the organization and, more than that, the *ethos,* of a nation that determines if its constitution bears any relation to reality. Different countries, with different traditions, have different approaches to the written law of the land.

The British, as we know, do not even *have* a written constitution. Nor do they seem to need one: The common law and the rooted customs of that nation apparently assure that nothing will be done in practice that violates the Britons' sense of personal freedom. Not a piece of parchment, but a general consensus, gives unity and coherence.

There is a joke — and more than a joke — that has long made the rounds in Soviet-controlled Eastern Europe:

"In England, everything that is not prohibited is permitted. In Germany, everything that is not permitted is prohibited. In France, everything that is prohibited is permitted. In the U.S.S.R., everything that is permitted is prohibited."

How the people feel about laws — all the way up to and including constitutional restraints — profoundly affects prohibitions and permissions in every area of life. There was no way the American public was going to obey Prohibition, even though it was a constitutional amendment. A law that goes against the grain might as well be written in water.

Comparing constitutions alone is an exercise in legal futility. The Italian people are not going to pay their income tax as dutifully as Americans do; and the Iron Curtain countries are going to continue to have a thriving black market, no matter how illegal it may be proclaimed.

Despotisms always crumble, although sometimes they are replaced by other despotisms, as in Iran. Revolutions tend to become even more repressive than the regimes they overthrow, as in France. The Germans were easy game for Hitler, because their key word was *obedience;* the looseness of the Weimar Republic made them nervous, and the nervous system of a nation is the best index of its behavior.

Lies Are Not Easily Put to Rest

THERE IS ONLY ONE FLAW in the noble maxim "Truth, crushed to earth, will rise again." And it is a serious flaw.

Exactly the same may be said of a lie. Truth may win out in the end, but few of us ever live long enough to see the end. And a lie seems to have a thousand lives.

The hate-mongers, for instance, are still peddling those fictitious "Protocols of the Elders of Zion," purporting to expose a sinister plot by international Jewry — although the document has been proved to be a blatant forgery time and again.

The phony Abraham Lincoln quotes also refuse to die. One that was revived as late as 1954 (and by no less than the then–postmaster general, Arthur E. Summerfield) and has been reprinted dozens of times by conservative propagandists went as follows: "You cannot bring about prosperity by discouraging thrift. You cannot strengthen the weak by weakening the strong. You cannot help the wage earner by pulling down the wage payer. You cannot further the brotherhood of man by encouraging class hatred. You cannot help the poor by destroying the rich." (This persistent hoax was finally traced to a leaflet distributed by the "Committee for Constitutional Government," one of whose leaders was Edward A. Rumely, who had served time as a German agent.)

Another false Lincoln quotation is actually chiseled into the stone entrance of the New York *Daily News* building: "God must have loved the common people; He made so many of them." There is not the slightest record that Lincoln ever said this.

Unfortunately, the power of a lie often seems to overcome the strength of truth, and, crushed to earth, the lie shows as much durability. We believe what we want to believe, what we like to believe, what suits our prejudices and fuels our passions. And if we can attach a great name to the sentiment, so much the better.

Some lies perpetuate themselves so long that they become part of a national mythos, like Washington's cherry tree and William Tell's apple and King Arthur's sword in the stone. With time, fact and fiction blur, and the fiction tends to become the prevailing "truth."

Charles S. Peirce, an American philosopher, once defined *truth* as "that which is fated ultimately to be believed by everyone," but ultimately is a long time, and meanwhile lies refuse to be buried, and their resurrections walk around as the most mischievous of ghosts.

Long summer vacations were begun in America when children were needed to work on the farms; they are continued in our urban society largely because teachers require this period in order to recuperate.

■

Politicians should be barred from quoting Lincoln unless they can demonstrate that they are imitating him also.

Officials Live Far from Sources of Blight

IT WAS ON A BALMY JUNE AFTERNOON in 1858 that the wind suddenly turned, and the stench from the Thames river caused a rapid evacuation of the Houses of Parliament.

The members rushed out pell-mell, led by Disraeli, with a mass of papers in one hand and a pocket handkerchief clutched to his nose with the other, fleeing what *The Times* (London) described as a "pestilential odor."

Shortly after this nauseating incident, Disraeli, then chief of the Conservative Party, introduced a bill for financing of new sewage drains — eleven years after the establishment of the Metropolitan Commission of Sewers for that very purpose.

Thus has it always been. It is usually not until the movers and shakers themselves are personally affected that necessary reforms are made. As long as they can remove their presences from the sights and smells of industrialism, the noxious conditions are generally allowed to persist, despite public discomfort and even danger.

Little has changed in the century and a quarter since that day, except that both the discomfort and the danger have multiplied with the inevitable expansion of the industrial age. More people are now exposed to more environmental perils than ever before in history.

But, around the world, the people who are most exposed are not the ones most responsible. In the worst incident of its kind, at Bhopal, India, in December 1984, not a single executive of Union Carbide, or a high-level government supervisor of the plant, lived anywhere near the site of the calamity — or was even on hand when the tragic leak occurred.

Corporate and government officials domicile themselves in "good" neighborhoods, which is to say as far as possible from fetid smells, ugly sights, and potentially dangerous environments. In the event of a disaster, they are rebuked, or the companies are fined (which is considered a small part of "the cost of doing business"), but they are not customarily sent to prison, nor is their families' health jeopardized.

(Radicals may care to attribute this to the evils of capitalism, but conditions are not conspicuously different in communist countries, where the administrators and bureaucrats are fully as segregated from the common workers and are extended much the same living privileges as any ruling caste, Marxist or not.)

Industrialism has been both a blessing and a curse to modern society; but while the blessings have been widely distributed, the curse has fallen almost wholly upon those whose labor and income force them to live close to the sources of contamination. In this, more than in anything else, it is tragically true that one man's meat is another's poison.

The Dangers of "Reification"

ONE OF THE DEFINITIONS of *cant* given in Webster's is "hypocritically pious language." And nowhere do we find more cant than in the official statements of governments, no matter how democratic or despotic they may be in form.

Not long ago, for instance, Secretary of State George Shultz told the House Foreign Affairs Committee that the United States has a "moral duty" to prevent Nicaragua from becoming a permanent ally of the Iron Curtain countries.

Whether he is right or wrong about Nicaragua, what sticks in my craw is the reference to our "moral duty." Nations as such can have no moral duties, no morals of any kind. Only persons have morality.

One of the worst intellectual errors anyone can make is to reify a word. This means taking an ideal or an abstraction, like "nation," and viewing it as a concrete and material object. And then, usually, ascribing human traits and feelings to this abstraction.

Only people have feelings; geographic units do not. Only people have ethics; governments as such do not. States and governments have *interests,* and these interests change with changing conditions. This is why last year's "enemy" may easily become next year's "ally."

This is also why we can make overtures to Chinese communism and undertures to Soviet communism. Why we will support dictators of the right in preference to dictators of the left. Why we will stick our noses into one area of the world and leave another severely alone.

America is no different in this respect from any other nation, only a touch more self-deceptive about our past and our present. We have, it is true, behaved better than most nations, largely because we had our own New World that needed conquering and little time or energy for Old World struggles for dominance or hegemony.

But morality has nothing at all to do with it. The most moral country in the world may have been Great Britain, in terms of decency to its own citizens. But the Britons were beastly to the American patriots, ghastly to the populace of India, and vile toward the Irish for centuries.

It is impossible to reify a nation, except to endow it with attributes, good or bad, that properly belong only to persons. There are many "good" people in every "bad" nation, and many "bad" people in every "good" one. What happened to all those "treacherous Japanese," who are now among our principal allies and most prosperous trading partners?

As a people, we admire physical superiority, and nobody expects star athletes to scale down their performances to the common public level; but in feats of mental or cultural superiority, we tend to resent the level of achievement and condemn as "highbrow" the same proficiency we applaud on the playing field as "awesome."

Practical Subjects Are Philosophical at Base

MOST OF US make a sharp distinction between the subjects we call "practical" and those we label "philosophical," or the "concrete" and the "abstract." We also assume that practical matters are easy to describe and define, while the philosophical ones are difficult or impossible to make clear.

Take two separate lists of four common words each. On one list we have the terms *truth, liberty, justice,* and *equality.* On the other hand we have *asset, profit, capital,* and *reserve.*

Again, most people would be surprised to learn that the four concrete words on the second list are just as difficult to pin down as the four abstract words on the first list. The hard business terms are just as slippery and ambiguous as the soft philosophical ones.

The chief difference is that the commercial world makes believe that there is general agreement and understanding of the phrases it throws around so casually in its reports, statements, and accounting systems. The truth is, however, that the concepts used in finance are as much convenient fictions as cold facts.

In a recent book recommended by the distinguished British magazine *The Economist,* the author candidly discloses that accountants themselves are dubious about some of the basic notions of their profession, including all four of the familiar terms I listed above.

In the book *The Pocket Accountant,* the author confesses: "It turns out that to define what an accountant means by an *asset* is exceptionally difficult." As for *profit,* he continues, "accountants have been unsuccessful so far in finding an acceptable definition."

Capital turns out to be another "embarrassingly elusive" concept; while *reserves,* far from being, as the public thinks, "pots of cash squirreled away by companies," may be a dozen different things, depending on how the books are juggled to conform to or elude corporate tax laws.

Indeed, the book goes on, even that favorite touchstone of accountants, *true and fair,* is as nebulous a phrase as one will find in Hegel or Kant. Another book published at the same time, the authoritative *MacMillan Dictionary of Accounting,* calls it "an abstraction or philosophical concept," adding that "the meaning of the concept can remain the same while the content given to it can change."

Accounting is one of the oldest and most "practical" of disciplines, going back to the Babylonian Empire. Yet in all those centuries, the experts cannot agree on what they are talking about. Keep that in mind the next time you are tempted to jeer at "mere philosophy."

Opposing Principles Help Balance Society

I DEVOUTLY WISH we could get rid of two words in the popular lexicon: *liberal* and *conservative.* Both are beautiful and useful words in their origins, but now each is used (and misused) as an epithet by its political enemies.

Liberal means liberating — it implies more freedom, more openness, more flexibility, more humaneness, more willingness to change when change is called for.

Conservative means conserving — it implies preserving what is best and most valuable from the past, a decent respect for tradition, a reluctance to change merely for its own sake.

Both attributes, in a fruitful tension, are necessary for the welfare of any social order. Liberalism alone can degenerate into mere permissiveness and anarchy. Conservatism alone is prone to harden into reaction and repression. As Lord Acton brilliantly put it: "Every institution tends to fail by an excess of its own basic principle."

Yet, in the rhetoric of their opponents, both *liberal* and *con-*

servative have turned into dirty words. Liberals become "bleeding hearts"; conservatives want "to turn the clock back." But sometimes hearts *should* bleed; sometimes it would profit us to run the clock back if it is spinning too fast.

Radical, of course, has become the dirtiest of words, flung around carelessly and sometimes maliciously. Today it is usually applied to the left by the right — but the right is often as "radical" in its own way.

The word originally meant "going to the roots" and was a metaphor drawn from the radish, which grows underground. We still speak of "radical surgery," which is undertaken when lesser measures seem futile. The American Revolution, indeed, was a radical step taken to ensure a conservative government, when every other effort had failed.

Dorothy Thompson was right on target when she remarked that her ideal was to be "a radical as a thinker, a conservative as to program, and a liberal as to temper." In this way she hoped to combine the best and most productive in each attitude, while avoiding the pitfalls of each.

Society is like a pot of soup: It needs different, and contrasting, ingredients to give it body and flavor and lasting nourishment. It is compound, not simple; not like wine that drugs us, or caffeine that agitates us, but a blend to satisfy the most divergent palates.

Of course, this is an ideal, an impossible vision never to be fully realized in any given society. But it is what we should aim at, rather than promoting some brew that is to one taste alone. It may take another thousand years to get the recipe just right. The question is: Do we have the time?

It seems to me that the most important maxim Americans can keep in mind in this tremulous era was expressed a century ago by the great German historian, Jacob Burckhardt: "Beware the terrible simplifier!"

Pornography Is in the Eye of the Beholder

WHAT IS CALLED "PORNOGRAPHY," like beauty, seems to be in the eye of the beholder. There is no objective way of defining it that will cover all tastes — much like its sister-word, *obscenity*, with which the courts have vainly wrestled for centuries.

The latest assault on pornographic material was made recently, through the side door, in Minneapolis, when the city council passed an ordinance that defined it as a form of "sexual discrimination against women." The bill was promptly (and properly) vetoed by the mayor on the grounds that its vagueness and broadness failed to meet constitutional guidelines.

We might say about pornography what St. Augustine said about time: "If nobody asks me what time is, I know what it is; but if somebody should ask me, then I do not know what it is."

Likewise, I know pornography when I see it, and I despise it, both in verbal and pictorial form. But I am unable to define it to general satisfaction. What seems clearly pornographic to me might seem only mildly vulgar to you, and vice versa. These perspectives change with the times, for they are as much esthetic as they are social and moral.

It is a truism to observe that in my grandmother's day, people were shocked and offended when a skirt was lifted up to the calf. And in my day, moviegoers would have been equally appalled to see an unmarried couple even sitting on the same bed, and fully dressed. I never believed that explicit sexual scenes could be portrayed on the screen, and am still taken aback — but my children and their friends mostly shrug them off as "boring."

When *Playboy* first came out, much of the public was outraged at its "daring"; now, some decades later, it seems quite tame compared with its bolder rivals. Sexual morality, unlike its ethical superstructure, is a temporal and relative matter, changing with the tides of fashion.

This is why "crusades for decency" always fail: There is no permanent and objective way to define decency in any precise language — and the essence of law is that it must set precise limits, or it is invalid and unenforceable.

Every person, every group, every community, has its own level of acceptance and tolerance and rejection of what it considers indecent. But freedom of expression — however distasteful — is an interstate commodity, and no local or provincial government can bar such expression within its precincts. We may wince at pornography, but it is far better to have our sensibilities violated than our liberties curtailed by the most censorious elements in the population.

The Catch-22 of Being Gay

THE HOMOSEXUAL IN OUR SOCIETY — whether you approve of him or not — is enmeshed in a Catch-22 that makes the army version look positively benign.

Consider the case of John Green, a fifty-year-old electrician, who is suing the Central Intelligence Agency for $1 million. Green was fired from his job, and his five government security clearances were lifted, when he admitted to being gay.

Now, it is not a crime to be a homosexual in our society, but it might as well be. Green was bounced because the CIA (as well as other security forces) believes that gays are more susceptible to being blackmailed than straights are.

The official fear is that the threat of "exposure" might pressure the closet gays to trade classified material in exchange for silence about their tendency. But why are gays more likely to be the targets of blackmailers? Because if they are disclosed as such, they will be fired from sensitive jobs. This is the Catch-22.

If nobody much cared who was gay and who was not, the potential blackmailers would lose all their leverage. If our national attitude was "So what?" then the gays would be no more of a "security risk" than any straight male who might succumb to the blandishments of a seductive female foreign agent.

But since we do seem to care, and since thousands of gays are afraid to proclaim their true identity, our very attitude of intolerance generates the "risk" in hiring them for military-industrial positions of trust. In effect, we force them to hide, and then penalize them for hiding.

All we have to do is to change our archaic attitude, to bring it in line with most other civilized countries, and then quite automatically the homosexual is no longer any more fearful of being "exposed" than anyone else. And, just as automatically, once this fear of stigma is removed, the risk of blackmail evaporates like a puff of smoke.

(Actually, and historically, heterosexual men have proved to be far greater security risks in the spy system, bartering secrets for feminine favors, for greed, for revenge, or for political fanaticism.)

Mr. Green seems to have a good case against the CIA, especially since he didn't even bother to lie to the agency about his sexual proclivity when he was asked to provide a reference for a friend. He is not even subject to dismissal on a charge of perjury.

If a man is straight enough to admit he isn't straight, who in the world would try to blackmail him? This is the only way out of the Catch.

No society can be considered civilized unless tenderness is viewed as an integral part of manliness, and not alien to it.

■

The chief test of civilization is the amount of "difference" it is willing to tolerate and absorb; the one characteristic of all primitive societies is a horror of diversity.

"Not Proven" Verdict for Ambiguous Cases

I HAVE WRITTEN BEFORE about the Scottish legal verdict of "not proven," and its usefulness if we were to incorporate it into the American courtroom system. The criminal trial of John DeLorean was a classic example of this need.

What the jury's verdict of "not guilty" meant was that the government had not proved its case or had tried to prove it by means that were beyond permissible legal limits.

The prosecution deserved this rebuke, in my opinion, and DeLorean should not have been convicted on its evidence. But, at the same time, a verdict of "not guilty" seems to be going too far in the other direction. The defendant should not have left the courtroom smelling like a rose, when the odor he gave off was distinctly rancid.

The Scottish verdict of "not proven" was made to order for cases of this sort. It says, in effect, "We cannot convict a man on this kind of ambiguous evidence, but on the other hand, we do not feel comfortable in pronouncing him 'not guilty,' so that he is free of all charges."

I suspect that DeLorean is in for a lot of trouble on other counts, civil if not criminal, and he doubtless faces years of bitter litigation about the disposal of funds that were earmarked for the production of his motor car.

The jury in the dope-dealing case obviously wanted to reprimand the government for its dubious and shabby tactics; and the only way it could do this under our system was by rendering a "not guilty" verdict. This tended to make something of a hero out of the defendant and even to "vindicate" his actions in the eyes of many people.

There are numerous cases of this kind, in which a jury in America has only a black-or-white choice when confronted with a large gray area, where facts remain undetermined, and an ultimate judgment has to be suspended, even though grave doubts exist about the defendant's conduct and activities.

Here the "not proven" verdict manages to accomplish two goals at once: It rejects a prosecution based on insufficient or improper evidence, while at the same time it prevents the accused from claiming "innocence" of all wrongdoing and leaves a stain on his character.

Too many of our known criminals slip through the meshes of the law by technical devices and must be legally acquitted, even though the jury is morally certain that they are malefactors.

To ease the frustration of the public and to brand these men with the stamp of disapproval, the shadow of a "not proven" verdict seems most appropriate to follow them in the future, signifying both a respect for the law and a deep skepticism about their probity.

Honesty Not the Best Policy for Winning Votes

IN A RARE BURST OF CANDOR, the campaign manager for a successful senatorial candidate in 1984 admitted in an interview that his man was difficult to manage "because he had this penchant for answering questions and telling the truth."

Obviously, these are two of the biggest no-nos for candidates of whatever party or persuasion. You may have noticed in the preelection debates how the contestants almost always avoided answering pointblank questions put to them by their opponents.

They would slide almost imperceptibly from the question to their own prearranged and memorized version of the issue, as though they had flipped a card in their brain and were repeating what they wanted to get across, regardless of the specific issue that was raised.

For the plain fact is that all candidates are confronted by unanswerable questions, because no one political position can satisfy all of the constituency, and the whole point of a staged debate is to woo as many different constituencies as possible, not to alienate them with hard cold facts they do not care to hear.

As the old politico put it a century ago: "Candidates solicit money from the rich, and votes from the poor, on the pretext of protecting each from the other."

It is a melancholy observation that the only (very few) candidates who told the truth, the whole truth, and nothing but the truth in their speeches and advertisements were the ones who had absolutely no hope of winning, and therefore had nothing to lose. (I am not referring here, of course, to the fanatics of extreme left or right, who will say anything to inflame the electorate.)

A candidate for office who will answer questions, directly and fully and honestly, is a menace to his party and a nightmare to his campaign directors. He will have to admit inconsistencies and contradictions in his party's stands; he may have to tell his listeners that they must bite the bullet, when all they want to do is chew the fat.

Please do not accuse me of being cynical, because everyone who has been involved in a political campaign knows that, while the public imagines it wants the facts, what it really wants are assurances that its hopes and dreams will not be punctured by harsh reality.

A "penchant for telling the truth" can cripple a candidate's chances faster than being caught *in flagrante delicto* with the governor's wife. In a campaign, you don't answer questions — you deflect them, most usually with questions of your own that the opponent can't answer either.

We may agree in the abstract that "we want the best man to win" in an athletic contest, but actually most of us want our man to win, whether or not he is best.

Legalized Gambling Requires a Moral Society

THE TROUBLE WITH MOST discussions and disagreements is that they are largely conducted in a vacuum. Take, for instance, the question of legalized gambling. Are you for it or against it?

This is pretty much a meaningless question in the abstract. Where is it going to be legalized, and how is it going to be supervised and controlled? To whom will the revenues go, and how will they be allocated?

Consider legalized gambling as it exists in Great Britain, and then think of applying it to the United States. These are two wholly different matters: I would find it agreeable in Great Britain but completely unacceptable in America. Put simply, the British can be trusted to run it honestly; we cannot.

The English are among the most avid gamblers in the world; almost every adult is what they call a "punter" and takes a regular flutter on the horses, the pools, or the football games. The nation enjoys a healthy financial rake-off from these pursuits, with hardly a breath of scandal. Neither their police nor their politicians engage in the hanky-panky that is all too familiar with us.

The British betting commissioner (what we call a "bookie") is licensed, honest, and free of prior taint or illicit influence. There is no "fix" and few "connections" in Britain's legal and judicial systems.

Transpose this scene to the United States, and who is naïve enough to believe that it would retain any of its pristine innocence? All we have to do is look at the history of Las Vegas, and the shorter though equally lurid saga of Atlantic City. The kind of people who would be running and overseeing casinos and betting-shops would be a thousand light-years in integrity from their British counterparts.

Consider also the caliber of our politicians in contrast to that of our English cousins — not to mention their heavy influence on the regulatory commissions, the inspectors, the collectors, and the police departments themselves. Does anyone imagine that legalized gambling would be anything but another scam perpetrated upon the public?

We are not good enough, as a political entity, to be able to afford the luxury of this pleasure, or weakness, as you may view it. It takes a more moral society than ours to engage freely in an activity that can so easily be demoralized; it requires a more incorruptible body of public servants to administer a system so easily corrupted. The smell of money is simply too powerful a lure in American political noses.

There is no need to make the cynical assumption that "all politicians are crooked" in our country; most of them are not, at least in any overt sense. But there are enough who are, or who can be persuaded to look the other way in exchange for a favor, to guarantee that legalized gambling here would swell the private treasury of officials more than the public coffers. And you can bet on that.

A Nation's Best Critics Are Its Intellectuals

THE UNITED STATES is recognized, if not by itself, by most cultivated foreigners, as a resolutely anti-intellectual country. We regard our intellectual class with negligence, if not outright disdain, as individuals of little effect or influence on mundane matters.

Yet if we look at repressive countries, such as the Soviet Union on the left or Iran on the right, we find that it is not the ordinary citizen — the businessman or farmer or mechanic or policeman — who is making any protest against repression, but almost solely the intellectuals.

It is the writer, the painter, the musician, the scientist, or academician who is making waves, leading protests, being jailed or exiled, and fleeing his native land to breathe a freer air.

Even in Poland, where Lech Walesa is the leading dissident, there are a dozen intellectuals for every labor leader who has taken his stance. In Iran, it is the creative people of the educated class who have gone underground or fled the tyranny of the mullahs.

It is the function of the intellectual in any society not to be an uncritical "patriot" of the regime but rather to point out the flaws and discrepancies between what a nation professes and what it actually practices. For no nation lives up to its public statements.

If we pride ourselves on being an "open" society, in distinction to the totalitarian societies of both left and right, then we should cherish our intellectuals — or at least we should pay attention to them. This is far from saying that they are always right; but it is to say that we ignore their criticisms at our peril.

Other people want "freedom" simply to be let alone. For creative people in the arts and sciences, freedom is as necessary as the air they breathe. Without it, their inspiration dries up, and they become mere vassals or tools of the state — or, even worse, prostitutes, trading their ideas for a dubious "security" or a precarious "status."

The mental and social health of a nation depends upon the amount of variety, of diversity, of controversy and contention it not only permits but encourages. Most citizens are too busy making a living to engage in these activities; the intellectual, the artist, the visionary, all those who march to a different drummer, are invaluable for providing society with a corrective lens for its national myopia.

The intellectuals can be wrong, of course — but we must give them the right to be wrong, and the attention and respect that is due to men and women who live not merely for today, but for a more beneficent future. Fallible as some may be, they are almost the only eyes and ears of tomorrow.

If He's Not Guilty, Why Is He in Court?

EVER SINCE OUR FOUNDING, it has been one of the cornerstones of the American legal system that a defendant is innocent until he is proved guilty — unlike, for instance, the French system, where the opposite is assumed.

Nevertheless, while our public pays lip service to this precept, our hearts remain wedded to a quite different maxim that has nothing to do with the law: "Where there's smoke, there's fire."

Most of us are not too unlike the old farmer called for jury duty, who explained how he voted: "I look at the fellow they bring in, and I say to myself, 'If he's not guilty, what's he doing here in court?' And then I cast my vote."

While it may be factually true that up to 90 percent of defendants in a criminal case are guilty, they are not always guilty of what they are indicted for, and the evidence against them is not always conclusive beyond a reasonable doubt.

These considerations are not overriding in the emotional matrix of a trial, particularly if it has attracted large public attention. Juries, no less than the general public, are influenced as much by the position, the appearance, and the bearing of the defendent as by the hard facts — and if they don't like the cut of a man's jib, they find it easy to justify their verdict.

Even before a trial, or after someone has been legally acquitted, public perceptions of his probable guilt or innocence are shaped by his personality "aura," as it were. To cite two instances in the not distant past, both Edwin Meese and Bert Lance are regarded by many, if not most, to have behaved improperly, if not illegally, although neither has been found guilty of anything in a court of law.

The shadow cast by Lance's manipulations will follow him throughout his career, and no court decision can move him back into the sunlight. The public's nose for the unsavory may

here be keener than the judge's eye for technical violations —
but it signally fails to grasp the distinction between a "sin" and
a "crime."

We pride ourselves on being "a nation of laws, not of men,"
but there is more form than substance, more illusion than
reality, in this belief. If someone with a record as a pick-
pocket is accused of murder, we are far more prone to accept
his guilt than that of a man with no prior record, although
pickpockets commit murder as infrequently as the average
nonfelon.

"Where there's smoke, there's fire" may be a useful adage
for a householder, but it is a dangerous one for a juror — especially when many of the fumes, as in the DeLorean case, are
generated by the prosecution.

*Speaking of proverbs, "A penny saved is a penny got" is most
often cited as a piece of prudent wisdom; but James Thomson,
who quoted the line, called it a "scoundrel maxim" in the very
next line, condemning those whose main goal in life is a narrow
commercial interest.*

■

*When the bulk of students in any country protests against their
government's policies, that government would be wiser to reexamine the policies than to repress the dissent; for a nation that
loses the allegiance of its young people faces a dubious future.*

■

*Customarily, it is not until one becomes a victim that one stops
blaming other victims for their plight.*

■

*History repeats itself, but in such cunning disguise that we never
detect the resemblance until the damage is done.*

Addressing the Different Needs of Man

WE ARE WRONG, I think, in dividing human societies into the "primitive" and the "civilized," for these categories do not correspond to the conflicting psychological needs and demands of the human person.

A more realistic division would be between the "traditional" or "corporate" and the "modern" or "individualistic." Each of these kinds of cultures offers something essential to a sense of identity, and each deprives one of something that seems equally essential.

The whole history of Western civilization is the steady movement toward the individualistic style of life. From the beginning, Europe and then the New World marched relentlessly in the direction of more autonomy for the person, more individual rights and freedoms, and the weakening of social and communal controls.

The traditional societies of the East, with their corporate character, have been waging a rear-guard battle against this modern tendency; but until now at least it has seemed as futile as the efforts of the Native Americans to preserve their way of life against the encroachments of the white pioneers and settlers.

What we are beginning to learn, if only dimly, is that each of these distinct styles brings its own blessings and its own burdens to a society, and you get nothing without paying a price for it. Until now, we have believed that we paid a relatively small price for the benefits of modernity and individual freedom; but mounting evidence seems to bear out the suspicion that we have lost as much as we have gained.

The traditional closely knit culture restrained the individual, but it also provided him with a sense of belonging, both to his community and to the forces of nature. The "alienation" that Marx observed in modern society was as much the result of industrialism as of capitalism. Loneliness and estrangement are the deep side effects of a rampaging individualism.

How can a traditional society promote personal freedom, and how can a modern society preserve cohesion and affiliation among its members? Traditional societies make people narrow in their sympathies and rigid in their responses; modern atomistic societies make people indifferent in their sympathies and selfish in their responses.

This may well be the most important question we have to answer in the twenty-first century; thus far, we are not even asking it.

Freedom Not to Pray

IF ONE STUDIES THE HISTORY of Colonial America, it becomes sadly evident that the emigrants who fled to our shore to escape persecution, and to set up communities of their own, did not really value freedom at large any more than did the societies they left behind.

For, with the singular exception of Providence, Rhode Island, they did not generally permit any more freedom of conscience to their own heretics and dissidents than they themselves had been permitted in the past. The settlers in the New World were just as harsh and punitive toward their minorities as anybody else.

We must reluctantly conclude that what most people want when they say they want freedom is freedom only for the orthodoxy of their own faith, whatever it may be. It took more than a century for us to expand this concept to include, and protect, the people who held unpopular views on religion, morality, or social organization — such as the Mormons, for one.

Lord Acton prescribed that the truest test of any civilization is the way it treats its minorities, and while our country has had a better record than most over the long pull, we are still not quite sure that as much "freedom" ought to be extended to heresy as to orthodoxy.

This vestigial reluctance to tolerate all shades of thought and belief is largely responsible for the continuing tedious public debate on "prayer in the schools" that has taken up so much time so fruitlessly in the halls of Congress.

There remains a lingering prejudice that because those who profess to believe in a deity are more numerous than those who disavow such belief, therefore the will of the majority should prevail, and children should be permitted, if not overtly encouraged, to mumble a few phrases of obligatory devotion in secular classrooms.

I happen to share in the sense of divinity, but this is no reason at all to promote prayer in the classroom, or anywhere else under public auspices. It is not simply a question of "church versus state," but a question of good sense, good manners, and good citizenship.

If "freedom of conscience" means anything, it means freedom not to pray, not to be devout, not to follow the majority. It also means that conscience is a private matter, and that a person who chooses not to acknowledge a Maker is not infringed upon any more than the persons who pay reverence to one god or three or six and a half.

Most proponents of school prayers secretly if not openly yearn for uniformity, not diversity, of belief — a uniformity of their own particular creed. The kind of god they would project is an offense to a compassionate Creator.

While churches should certainly not pay income taxes, there is no legitimate reason that they should be exempt from government regulations that require other nonprofit organizations to account for the expenditure of contributions, and to document whether the contributions are spent for the actual purpose designated in fundraising appeals.

No Frontiers Left for Today's Dropouts

NINE PERSONS OUT OF TEN will tell you that we have compulsory education in America, but of course we do not. All we have is compulsory attendance. That is the most any country can have.

You can compel a child to attend school, more or less, but you cannot force him or her to get an education. If a youngster is not motivated from within, no curriculum, no teachers, no form of threat or persuasion will do more than place a warm body before a desk.

One of the problems we do not seem to recognize is the changing structure of society in the late twentieth century. In past eras, just as many children, I am convinced, were indifferent to or repelled by school, but it didn't make nearly so much difference then.

Young people who were physical and kinetic could find relatively unskilled work fairly easily. Or they could stay on the farm, dig in the mines, cut down the forests, lay the railroad tracks, or apprentice themselves to shopkeepers and artisans in any of a score of areas of trade.

This need has dried up beyond the imagination of our forebears. A literal revolution has taken place in occupations since the founding of our country: from some 90 percent self-employed to an equal proportion now working for some firm or corporation.

But, while this *bouleversement* has been taking place, the nature of people has not changed. Just as many boys and girls as ever are impatient with schooling, resentful of reading and calculating, and ready to kick over the traces and enter the "real world."

The real world, however, is not the one their grandparents or even their parents grew up in. It is a world that is highly synchronized to a technological beat. Products are not needed as much as services — and the services call for people who can read and write and count and comprehend the complexities of society.

There is no longer any room for a Huckleberry Finn —just as there would no longer be any room for a Mark Twain if he opted to remain a riverboat captain today, instead of an author. The "marginal" people have been squeezed out; you are either fully in society, or outside it, unless you have a special flair or talent.

These are bad days for square pegs, for all the holes are getting rounder and rounder. As our options narrow, those who drop out of school, for one reason or another, can find no frontier to escape to, no place to drop in to, as their ancestors could. For them, the only alternative to school is not the open road, but a blind alley.

The only attitude more distasteful than the arrogance of the old, who think that the young know nothing, is the arrogance of the young, who think that the old have forgotten what they once knew, if they ever knew it.

■

A communal catastrophe, calling for collective effort, seems to elicit two opposite responses at once: It brings out the best in good people — and the worst in bad people.

■

It always surprises me that so few parents realize that the best things you can give children, next to good habits, are good memories, which support and nourish a person for a lifetime; so many parents are busily engaged in instilling good habits at the expense of good memories, that the habits bring only a grim satisfaction in later life, as a substitute for joy.

Can We Reconcile Technocracy and Democracy?

IN A DEMOCRACY, in order for the citizens to make intelligent decisions, it is first necessary that they have access to all the relevant information pertaining to these decisions. This is axiomatic in every case.

But with the growing complexity and sophistication of modern armaments, governments feel it necessary to devise and develop military capability that must be kept secret from any potential enemy — which means it must be kept secret from the public as well.

This means that the citizens are barred from knowing what their own government is doing and planning, beyond what the government is inclined to tell them. Under the rubric of "national security," tremendous international insecurity may be built up by the military architects of the several nations.

We are then, in effect, being asked to have blind trust in our leaders — who may not be our leaders next year, or the year after, when the consequences of their build-ups may come to deadly fruition. We are being asked to invest blind confidence in their intelligence, their judgment, their foresight — and their good will.

This, however, is not how a democracy was meant to work. If ultimate power resides in the electorate, then the electorate must be in a position to determine matters of policy. But how can it rationally determine such matters if modern technology — quite apart from the secrecy involved — is so abstruse and technical that the average citizen can barely comprehend its implications?

This is a problem of looming dimensions that democracy has never before faced. In the past, armies confronted each other openly; weaponry was largely recognized and understood; offense and defense had clear lines of demarcation; and, most of all, none of the belligerents possessed the power to totally annihilate the enemy, civilians and all, ten times over, as we do today.

Whether one is for or against nuclear weapons, the fact remains that no one outside a small cadre of experts really comprehends the enormity of the next conflict, and even they cannot agree. How can we ordinary citizens tell if the doves are too alarmist or the hawks too ferocious? Their views are based on their political positions as much as on any objective assessment of the realistic risks and perils.

What are we to believe? To whom can we turn for counsel? Can we believe a government that has been less than candid with us in the past? Can we trust leaders who make out the best possible case for their position, and the worst possible case for their opponents? This is a matter that goes so far beyond politics that it dwarfs all partisan squabbles and overshadows all narrow sectarianism.

"For your own good, we cannot tell you everything you want to know." This is not the voice of democracy, but that of despotism, benevolent or not. If we sacrifice democracy in order to defend it, when will we ever get it back? And in what condition will it be, given the unimaginable cost of a global catastrophe?

Most voters who term themselves "independent" would be more honestly labeled as "disaffected."

■

We have now reached the age of "unlimited power" predicted nearly a century ago by Henry Adams; but we have neglected to heed his warning about "the effect of unlimited power on limited minds" and his farsighted anticipation of the madness of a nuclear arms race.

Law Both Liberates and Enslaves

ONE OF THE MOST PERPLEXING PARADOXES in the long history of the human race is the fact that we were not fully civilized until we began to live under the rule of law — and yet it is the law itself that now threatens to strangle us as mercilessly as Laocoon and his sons were done in by serpents.

The rule of law is perhaps the noblest work of man, allowing him to transcend his baser instincts and accommodate to a mutual agreement without violence or rupture. At the same time, the mechanism of law has turned from a means to an end, from a tool to a weapon that often resembles the ancient Juggernaut more than anything else.

It is too easy to take a cheap shot at the lawyers themselves, for they are nearly as much the victims as the culprits — overwhelmed by the increasing complexity and tortuosity and sinuosity of this looming monster we have created and cannot control.

Nobody is happy with the system we have evolved, even the beneficiaries, who have to hire more and more lawyers to protect and defend and interpret and elude the meshwork of legalism that constricts us in every aspect of our corporate, industrial, domestic, and civil lives.

Instead of simplifying and lubricating the mechanism of society, the law complicates and clogs up all the normal processes, impeding rather than facilitating its original goal, which is equity.

What is tragic in our current situation — a situation that is perhaps more aggravated in the United States than anywhere else in the modern world — is that the public, if it becomes impatient enough of the increasing perversions of the system, may decide to revert to our more atavistic instincts and, as it were, take the law into its own hands.

These hands have been bloodied through centuries of cruelty and superstition and prejudice and ignorance, which are always lurking barely an inch below the civilized veneer. We might not burn witches anymore, but there are a lot of other people we would like to burn, with less ecclesiastical sanction and more savage enthusiasm.

The law was conceived as something above men, but its history is a sad study in steadily lowered standards of manipulation and mastery by the strong against the weak, the cunning against the simple, and parasites against producers.

I fear for the whole fabric of law and jurisprudence, for I see nothing but anger, sullen resentment, and frustration in the public temper today — and when these are the prevailing passions, we know that the law will not be improved or reformed, but trampled, repudiated, and violated by a populist mob more blinded by the law's deficiencies than inspired by its ideals.

Public Needs Protection from the Police

IN ORDINARY CIRCUMSTANCES, big city police make out a plausible case that their hands are tied by niceties of the law, by technicalities, and by civil libertarians who seem to care more about the rights of criminals than the wrongs of victims.

The police ask to be made freer of legal limitations and judicial impositions on their actions and modes of operation. It all sounds so fair, so reasonable, so commonsensical that these brave men who "serve and protect" should not be handcuffed in their difficult duties.

Then, when we are almost persuaded, two policemen are shockingly killed in broad daylight and a massive manhunt begins for the culprits. Like a corps of commandos in an occupied country, scores of policemen sweep through the black neighborhood where the killings occurred, throwing all concepts of legal restraint to the winds.

They pick up anyone who even remotely resembles a description of the culprits, wantonly rough up innocent people, invade homes, bash down doors, and leave wreckage in their wake. Angry beyond bounds, they disdain to make even a pretense of working within the law, secure in the knowledge that no retribution, official or otherwise, will be visited upon them.

The American public likes its police, far more than European publics do (except for the British). We have not been subjected to strong-arm tactics as much as other nations have, by police acting as paramilitary forces to uphold a repressive or a revolutionary regime.

We tend to go along with their cheery slogan that they "serve and protect." We know they do a tough job and have traditionally been underpaid and subservient to political influences, especially in the big cities. And we sympathize with their complaint that the court system is clogged, cumbersome, and sometimes corrupt.

But then, whenever a real crisis ensues, whenever passions are aroused, they forfeit our sympathy by demonstrating that only fear of reprisal prevents them from taking the law into their own hands and violating the basic tenets of civil liberties in a free society.

Their behavior in such circumstances warns us that we cannot trust them to serve and protect everyone equally when the gloves are off, when they are reacting as outraged members of a corps and not as custodians of the law. We may call this conduct a "human failing," but so frail an excuse should not be invoked when men behave like beasts more than like human beings. Handcuffing the police may be the only way to prevent them from cuffing the public.

As long as peace is considered a passive condition, and not a perpetual activity, eras in which it prevails will remain only a breathing space between preparation for renewed conflicts.

We Need More Specialists in Law

WE TEND TO LAUGH at the proliferation of specialties in the medical profession — like the legendary doctor who treats only the *left* nostril — but while it may in some cases be carried to absurd extremes, there is no doubt that the growing complexity of medicine makes this tendency almost inevitable, for the sake of the doctor and of the patient.

Actually, one can fault the legal profession for failing to do the same and for greedily trying to bite off more than it can chew. The fact is that the law in America has become just as complicated as — and even more contradictory than — the field of medicine.

One man can hardly digest the corpus of federal law alone, much less state law and all the diverse subdivisions of the legal and judicial process. Doctors don't try to practice heart surgery and dermatology at the same time, and it is just as fatuous for a lawyer to pretend to a client that he can adequately handle any old case that comes along.

A general practitioner in medicine will not hesitate to refer a patient to a specialist, because he knows that the patient will return to him for ordinary treatment; but a lawyer who refers a potential client to a specialist is likely never to see him again and simply loses a fee permanently, which tends to dampen his ardor.

While the law profession needs a solid core of generalists to handle everyday matters, it should also require law schools and bar associations to encourage and recognize more specialization, so that the ignorant and confused client does not waste his time and money dealing with an attorney who knows no more about his particular kind of litigation than a hog knows about Sunday.

Yet, apart from a handful of truculent trial lawyers and another handful of austere corporate attorneys, the bulk of lawyers in this country advertise a laundry list of legal competences that would defy the combined talents of Holmes, Brandeis, Darrow, and Daniel Webster. Nobody would go to a podiatrist for a brain-scan, but this may be exactly what you are getting when you visit a lawyer cold.

In the British legal system, a solicitor prepares your case, and a barrister pleads it, and each has been trained specially for his task. It is sensibly assumed there that nobody can do both well — and, moreover, the experienced solicitor selects a barrister for you, based on his good knowledge of the right man for the right case.

Lawyers here should pass "boards," as doctors do, and become certified in a specialty, so that the client with anything but a run-of-the-mill case could knock on the proper door and be assured of competence, if not brilliance. Many a man behind bars knows it now.

Capital Punishment Hurts Society More Than It Hurts Victims

LET ME TRY TO EXPLAIN by an analogy, as simply and clearly as I can, why people like me are against capital punishment. It seems to me that our motives and our reasons are grossly misunderstood.

Last fall one of my sons, as he usually does, took part in the deer-hunting season in Wisconsin. While I would not kill a deer myself, I realize the practical reasons for thinning out the herd for the ultimate benefit of the deer themselves.

But while some hunters go out in ones and twos to get their bag, others go out in dozens or more, like a posse. They spread out, sequester a group of deer in a thicket, then slaughter them as the deer come bounding out of the brush.

This is not sport, it is a massacre. This time, a fifteen-year-old boy went out with them for the first time. He wounded a big one, but did not kill him, so a man went up and slit the deer's throat, so that the head would not be "ruined" for the boy's trophy.

My objection is not so much to what is done to the deer as to what is done to the boy. For one thing, it desensitizes him to cruelty; for another, it justifies whatever is done to win your "antlers"; and for another, it turns killing into a casual, callous, thoughtless act.

Likewise, in terms of capital punishment for humans, my objection again is not so much to what is done to the criminal as to what is done to society, to the citizens who execute him. My objection is not sentimental but humanitarian in the broadest sense: I am concerned about what effect legal killing has upon the humans who perpetrate it.

It is terribly easy to become hardened to this, because it is a simple "solution" to a complex problem (even though it is no solution at all). And once a society becomes accustomed to killing its murderers, there is no logical line that can be drawn anywhere against killing others.

Kidnapers, of course. Rapists, most likely. Terrorists, certainly. Army deserters in time of war. Everyone would have his own little list. Religious fanatics would like the state to kill heretics and atheists (and did so when they had the power). Political extremists would be pleased to kill dissenters (and do so everywhere around the world).

It is not a question of who "deserves" death, if anyone does. It is a question of so conditioning people that the state can justify executions in one category or another. Moreover, as we all know, it is the poor, stupid, half-crazy, desperate, or depraved individual who is executed, not the master criminal, who rarely sees the inside of a cell.

Capital punishment may not be unjust to the offender. It is, by its very nature, unjust to the character of a good society.

Terrorists Seek Transcendence

IT IS EASY to call terrorists crazy, and no doubt some of them, if not most of them, are. But this does not really explain why they are willing to do what they do, and to glory in it.

Chesterton pointed out many years ago, "When a man has found something which he prefers to life, he then for the first time begins to live." Most terrorists (as distinguished from mere mercenary assassins) have simply found something which they prefer to life.

In our eyes, of course, they have found the wrong thing and are duped or deluded or drunk with fanaticism. But this is not really the point; goals may differ, but it is only when we have found something larger than ourselves which we are willing to live for, and to die for if need be, that we come fully alive.

It would be desirable, of course, if our object were creative and affectionate rather than destructive and based on hate or vengeance. Most people, however, are not deep enough or broad enough to encompass such goals; rather, they dedicate their lives to a particular piece of land or a provincial flag or a partial cause.

Yet the psychological mechanism remains much the same: It is the willingness to work for, and be used by, a purpose beyond one's own ego that most fulfills the personality.

Both the best and the worst people are animated in this fashion. It may be a Hillary climbing Everest, or a Nelson aboard the *Victory,* or an Edith Cavell nursing soldiers, or anyone who feels most alive when he or she is living or risking or sacrificing for a goal greater than the satisfaction of one's own selfish wants.

Much pathology may be involved here, but also much nobility and saintliness. And quite apart from these rare extremes, it is true for the ordinary person that unless he or she has a reason for living beyond mere survival, there is a certain savor lacking in life.

Some people find it in their children, some in the arts, some in exploration, some in working for manifold charities and causes and crusades of various degrees of worth. Many do it to "lose" themselves in something; few are willing to lose everything.

Paradoxically, it is those most tightly wrapped in themselves, so preoccupied with preserving what they have, who are most prone to boredom and fear and anxiety and hypochondria. The terrorists are terrible because they are doing the wrong things for the right reasons; but, warped as they are, they are vivid proof of the old Latin maxim that the worst is a corruption of the best.

"Wings" Are for the Birds

THE WORST THING that ever happened in world politics took place in France long ago, when conservative members of Parlement were seated to the right of the chair, and liberal and radical members to the left. Since then, almost every European legislature has followed the same practice.

This arbitrary designation of "left" and "right" has persisted to our time and has done incalculable damage to our political thinking. It encourages us to label parties and factions without much regard to the policies they actually subscribe to or the changes they advocate.

We refer to Soviet Russia as a "left-wing" government, when in fact it has been more fascist than communist for the last forty years — although the fascists are called "right-wingers."

What are the new breed of Libertarians to be labeled as? They are radical in some ways, conservative in others, and moderate or neutral in still others. They fit comfortably into no traditional niche.

What about the "populist" parties that manage to combine a form of "socialism" with a sinister undercoating of "fascism"? Hitler's party, after all, called itself the National Socialist German Workers, and combined the worst elements of left and right in its appeal to the voters.

We now have something called the "radical right" in American politics, which ought to be a contradiction in terms. The right is supposed to be "conservative," but how do we distinguish this from "reactionary"? And when does a reactionary cease to be a conservative and become a right radical?

The so-called left is as divided and conflicted as the right, with differing forms of Marxism and socialism and hybrids of all kinds, each accusing the others of "treason" to the left. The Russian and the Chinese brands of "communism" (whatever that may mean today) are at swords' points as much as we and the Russians.

We are against communism but are staunch allies with a number of European "socialist" countries that consider themselves "left" even though they fear and oppose the leftism of the Soviet Union. And we are equally supportive of repressive "right-wing" governments in Central and South America.

It is all a hopeless tangle, with no clear lines of demarcation, and no consistency in terms of political principles and practices. "Wings" are not only left and right, but up and down and around and across — and only serve to confound the electorate, while their leaders keep on doing whatever they have to do to keep in power, flying on one wing or another.

The French say, "The more things change, the more they remain the same"; but it is equally true that the longer things remain the same, the more sudden and cataclysmic will the change be.

Nations Should Submit to the Rule of Law

IF YOU ARE NOT personally or politically involved in a conflict, you can see quite clearly that there is right and wrong on both sides. In most such disputes, we know that there is rarely an "innocent party."

Whether it is the Protestants and Catholics in Northern Ireland or the Israelis and PLO in the Middle East, or the Iranians and the Iraqis, we on the outside may not have as much *knowledge* of the ins and outs, but we do have sounder *judgment* about human conduct.

Distance may lend enchantment in some cases, but more often it lends a perspective that the participants are incapable of sharing. They are so involved in their parochial argument that all judgment is warped by passion, envy, hatred, revenge, and mourning.

If the world needs one thing, it needs a Court of Justice to which warring factions can repair, as individuals do when locked in intractable opposition. This has been the great development of civilization from primitive times when disputants made individual retribution.

But the great barrier to this rational solution is the overriding theory of sovereignty, by which each nation asserts and demands the right to judge — and judge alone — in its own case. And since each country wants to retain this right, for its own interests, no one is willing to submit to outside arbitration.

What seems perfectly plain to me is that there is no way out of this terrible box, and that as long as anarchy reigns among the nations of the world, there is no hope of anything resembling genuine peace — only one uneasy truce after another, followed by increasingly devastating wars one after another.

As individuals, we are willing to do this — indeed, we are

compelled by law to do this — but there is no law that encompasses the modern Leviathan. Each nation is a law unto itself and of course always decides each case in its own favor.

And this "favor" is usually in the interest of the regime or the politicians leading the country, more than it is in the interest of the ordinary citizen, who has to be emotionally whipped into a war fever by his leaders' painting the "enemy" as inhuman monsters bent on devouring us.

"Patriotism" is love of one's country; "nationalism" is the delusion that one's country is superior to all others and deserves better than the others. It is a collective egotism that no individual would assert for himself, except under the cloak of a national symbol.

We are still light-years away from a world government, which no doubt poses its own perils. But what rational alternative do we really have, when each decade it becomes more evident that the unrestrained sovereign ego points toward death while pretending to defend life?

An international police force to restrain disputing nations is ultimately the only answer to international violence; as Whitehead put it, "The only justification in the use of force is to reduce the amount of force necessary to be used."

■

Despotism is always bound to fail, for the reason given a century ago by Disraeli, when that shrewd prime minister observed: "No government can be long secure without a formidable opposition."

■

"Terrorism" is what we call the violence of the weak, and we condemn it; "war" is what we call the violence of the strong, and we glorify it.

Prevention Beats Punishment
in Handling Terrorists

WE WILL NOT BE ABLE to deal effectively with terrorism — except by brute force, which ultimately resolves nothing — until we begin to grasp the mood and the temper of fanatics who blow up embassies and hijack airplanes, killing innocent victims to obtain publicity.

It is tiresome to keep being fed the cliché that "one man's terrorist is another man's freedom fighter." This is not the proper distinction to make about them — for it is not their *motivation* that sets them apart so much as their methods and their madness.

A genuine "freedom fighter" does not indiscriminately slaughter innocents, men, women, and children alike. He may be willing to give up his life for a cause, but he is not ready to take other lives that have no real bearing on his cause.

Whatever may turn out to be the best way of coping with terrorism, it seems clear that swift and certain punishment of the culprits is no solution. When tried and convicted, or executed, terrorists become martyrs, inspiring suicidal imitation. Their fate serves more as a model than a deterrence — and is seen by their fellows as a passport to Paradise.

The question is not "How can they be stopped?" but "How can they be persuaded not to start?" And this question is more a matter of law than of politics or tactics.

All terrorists perceive an "injustice" that they feel cannot be removed or relieved by any legitimate means, and terrorism is almost always a last resort, when all else has failed.

The only possible way out of this fatal impasse lies not in an international pact to prosecute terrorism as much as an international effort to adjudicate and arbitrate these social ills and inequities before they suppurate and burst.

Of course there will always be injustice in the world, just as there will always be illness and infection. But while we have learned to take preventive measures against disease, we have done practically nothing to forestall the fury of partisans who lack an adequate Court of Appeal, with the power to enforce its decisions.

As long as there is no genuine law among and for nations, what rule can we legitimately invoke against the anarchism of embittered and blindly enraged patriots?

Terrorists are not rational — but we have no rational system for balancing and determining the demands of disenfranchised minorities. Until we devise a Court of International Justice that really works, terrorism can only be countered by a greater terrorism, without end. It is desperation that generates terrorism, not depravity.

Accusations Incriminate the Accusers Most

HOW CAN YOU JUDGE a regime or a government if you've never been there? One of the best, and most reliable ways, I have found, is to pay attention to the charges it brings against its protesting citizens.

Whenever a regime is in trouble and feels a need to defend its policies, it almost always engages in the same tired phrases of opprobrium as these: "Outside agitators," "chronic trouble-makers," "a dangerous element," "opponents of law and order," "malcontents," "disloyal and traitorous citizens," "subversive organizations," and all their synonyms.

These are among the standard vituperations the Soviet Union has hurled against its dissidents over the decades; and no less the Philippines, South Africa, Argentina, Chile, and a host of other repressive regimes.

Certainly in some cases there are revolutionary underground forces trying to undermine the established government, but such groups flourish only in fertile soil — when there is enough injustice and oppression to make legitimate complaints difficult or impossible. No people is naturally revolutionary; it takes a despotism like that of czarist Russia or an arrogant colonialism like that of eighteenth-century England to rouse the public.

"Law and order" is the overriding shibboleth of these tyrannies, great and small. What is omitted is that the "law" is the law of the ruling clique, and the "order" is the order imposed by fiat rather than by civil liberties and constitutional limits.

And every regime, left or right, uses the identical language and pretexts for cracking down on its dissidents. The old Bolsheviks who opposed Stalin's harshness were labeled "enemies of the state" when they were really enemies of the betrayal of the state by its evil cabal.

It must be admitted, however, that this is mostly the rhetoric of the right. The rhetoric of the left consists largely of such warm, moist words as *freedom* and *equality* and *justice,* which may cloak a potential oppression as great as is that it seeks to overthrow. This was the historic tragedy of the French Revolution.

A government is ultimately judged by what it does, but, well before that, it can be appraised, even by strangers, by how it treats and what it calls its opponents. When Marcos of the Philippines calls his foes "Communists," and you see thousands of merchants and shopgirls marching in the streets, you know this is hot air.

"By their fruits ye shall know them," the Scripture alerts us. In political terms, it is by their invectives that we can identify the real malefactors.

Systematic repression is the surest way a government turns its "moderates" into "extremists."

■

The kind of information a president decides to impart to the country tells us more about him than it does about the country.

Democracy Is Hard to Define

THE DEATH EARLIER THIS YEAR of my old friend and tutor, Richard McKeon, who was one of the great Greek and philosophy scholars of our time, reminded me of one of his few academic projects that came to naught.

As a U.S. delegate to UNESCO in 1949, he was among six intellectuals serving on a committee that was assigned to compose an acceptable definition of *democracy.*

After nearly a week of close study, proposals, and debate, the committee was forced to disband, with the acknowledgment that an agreement could not be reached. With the best of intentions and good will in the world, these six fine minds could not arrive at a common consensus about this word we fling about every day.

There should be a lesson for us in this — for *democracy* is a compound word, not a simple one. There is political democracy, there is economic democracy, there is social democracy, and belatedly we are learning there is something called sexual democracy.

What does, or should, that one word imply? Is political democracy effective without its economic counterpart? Is economic democracy meaningful without its political twin? Is sexual democracy feasible, given the traditional roles of males and females in the world?

Almost everybody uses the word affirmatively — the Russians as well as we — but when we disagree on how it is to be applied, we cannot even agree on the concept we are disagreeing about, because we mean different things by the same word.

There are even Americans who insist that the United States was not meant to be a democracy, but a republic. There are others who assert that it is incompatible with capitalism. And still others who equate it with the kind of individualism in which the devil takes the hindmost.

Some people think we have too much democracy; others that we have too little. The anarchists and libertarians look upon government as a mechanism that interferes with democracy; the liberals and radicals believe that government fosters a greater measure of "full" democracy.

Perhaps it is a word we ought to stop using so frequently and so casually — and so thoughtlessly. It is a banner everyone likes to walk under, like *freedom* and *justice,* which are equally incapable of agreement in a univocal definition.

A week was not long enough, even for the great minds, but we don't even give the term a moment's thought. We "clarify" butter to get the impurities out, but we don't think it's worth the trouble to clarify our thinking about a system we live under — and are willing to die for.

In a tornado, one must open the doors and windows, rather than shut them, for it is the disparity between outer and inner pressure that demolishes houses; and so it is in the drive for social equality, where closing our doors does not ensure safety, but invites destruction.

■

Freedom of speech in public is meaningless unless you have permitted yourself freedom of thought in private.

■

If fifty million consumers snub a product, we blame the product; if fifty million voters abstain from voting, why do we blame them instead of the "products" on the ballot?

The Price of Being American

SOME FRIENDS of mine returned from a vacation in the Caribbean last winter and complained about how expensive it was — the accommodations, the food, and all the incidentals.

I told them it reminded me of an old story I once heard about the time King George I was taking a journey to Hanover. On the way, he stopped at a village in Holland for a short rest. While fresh horses were being readied, the king asked for two or three eggs. The charge on his bill was 200 florins, a truly outrageous sum.

He protested mildly while paying, with the words, "Eggs must be scarce around this place." The innkeeper smiled, "Pardon, sire, eggs are plentiful enough — it is kings that are scarce."

The price Americans pay abroad is the price for being an American. We have been known so long and so widely as the richest people on earth that it would be absurd to suppose that other peoples would not want to take advantage of our affluence.

Their attitude is not entirely a matter of envy or greed but is often a reaction that is conditioned by our own attitude in foreign countries, which is a curious combination of pity and contempt for native values and standards.

Nor has it changed much in recent years, despite the growth of overseas travel. From Mexico City to Rome, I have sat in restaurants or cafés and seen Americans peel off a roll of bills before a waiter, asking insolently, "How much is that in *real* money?" when presented with a tab in pesos or lire or any currency cheaper than ours.

Now world economists tell us that the distribution of wealth is beginning to shift, and the United States may enter the twenty-first century as a diminished financial power. Japan and the Common Market in Europe and the OPEC nations may very well be surpassing us in productivity and eventually in per capita income.

This may not be entirely a bad thing for us, socially, spiritually, and emotionally, however it may pinch a little economically. As a rich uncle among countries, we have been more respected than loved, and we tend to be puzzled and hurt at our lack of international popularity.

But in every century, the dominant nation has been regarded with the same combination of disdain and admiration. We were fortunate in having had a whole continent to develop and exploit, and that era seems to be dwindling to a close.

We may be forced to look inward now, and examine our values, rather than outward and count our assets. This may or may not improve our morals; it is bound to improve our public manners.

"Great" Men Are Often Bad

LORD ACTON'S FAMOUS DICTUM that "Power tends to corrupt ..." reminds me that while every schoolboy knows this phrase, hardly anyone is aware of the line that follows it: "Great men are almost always bad men."

And this was hardly original with him. Two centuries earlier, Thomas Fuller wrote, "Great and good are seldom the same man." If we look at the long tapestry of history, we find that for every one Washington or Lincoln, mankind has been cursed with a dozen Attilas and Napoleons and Hitlers.

Men actually called "Great" — like Peter and Alexander — have visited some of the most dreadful calamities not only upon their enemies but upon their own people as well. They spilled more blood for their own temporary glory and power than a good great man like Gandhi could have saved in a hundred years.

Nations clamor for, and adulate, strong leaders; but strength is far more often exercised on behalf of dominance than of justice, of aggression and conquest than of benevolence or mercy. As Shakespeare expressed it: "O! it is excellent to have a giant's strength; but it is tyrannous to use it like a giant."

We want great men to lead us, but they more often lead us into temptation than deliver us from evil. We most appreciate those leaders who can bind us together in a feeling of fellowship — but this fellowship is almost always directed against some rival fellowship, because solidarity thrives on conflict and disintegrates without a felt "enemy."

Power corrupts not merely because it enjoys the exercise of power, but because one of the most effective ways to retain it and to consolidate it is by rallying the troops against some convenient outsider who can be perceived, or projected, as a threat. In our time, Hitler was the consummate master of this tactic, playing like a virtuoso on the repressed emotions of the German people after their shattering defeat in World War I.

On a tiny scale, we could see this happening last year, with the U.S. invasion of Grenada, which was approved by 70 percent of Americans, and enormously bucked up our national mood, even though most dispassionate observers (including our allies) recognized it as a psychological propaganda plot without the slightest shred of legality or even common sense.

This is the kind of thing that populaces want from their leaders. We soured on the Vietnam expedition because we were losing, not because we felt it was wrong; we would have rejoiced over a speedy victory, regardless of the deeper issues involved. In this moral respect, all nations, and all peoples, are more alike than different.

Politicians in office object to a "leak" only when it comes from an unauthorized source, and not their own; as James Reston once observed: "A government is the only known vessel that leaks from the top."

There Is More to Life Than Economics

WHEN WE LOOK AT A COUNTRY like Russia, it seems clear that you can't take an economic system and make a total way of life out of it. Even if Marxism worked in the economic realm (and there is little indication that it does), it seems a monstrous perversion to turn it into a religion, a science, an art, and even a form of psychology, as the Russians do.

Yet we seem incapable of turning this picture around and looking at our own economic system in the same dispassionate way. If we did, we might begin to see something of the mirror-image we find in Russia.

That is, even if capitalism, or private enterprise, works in the economic realm (and the final returns are far from in yet), it also seems a cruel distortion to insist upon a competitive system for all other aspects of life, as though everything we do is a business.

The great evil in collectivism is that it leads to a diminution of personal responsibility and initiative; what belongs to everybody belongs to nobody. Conversely, the besetting sin of individualism is that it soon degenerates into privatism: What I can do for myself comes first, and the community comes last, if at all.

But you cannot transform an economic system into a philosophy of life without deforming and corrupting the nature of man. The nature of man is twofold: As a person, he is both an individual and part of a collectivity. The two must interact, with equal justice given to both sides of this delicate equation. If we are only collective, we become little better than ants; if we are only individualistic, we become little better than sharks.

It is easy for us to see what happens to people in the Russian matrix: all becomes dull, drab, uniform, and spiritless. It is less easy for us to see what happens in a society that deifies competition: all becomes predatory, private, and ruthless if necessary. Winning comes to mean everything, no matter how; and charity becomes a poor substitute for justice.

No economic system of any kind is self-justifying. All must be justified, by their fairness, their compassion, their legacy to the future as well as their allegiance to the past. If a system is not informed by honor and decency, it is rotten, no matter how rich or powerful it becomes in the world. And it must fall, as all such have.

The world of nature is one of both competition and mutual aid, in a nice balance that promotes the interests of all. Humankind has not yet found this proper equilibrium, and until we do it is a tragic mistake to suppose that our self-preservation is either the way of the ant or the way of the shark.

Newspapermen Have Clean Noses

MY EXPERIENCE MAY NOT EQUIP ME to speak for the other "media" (a term I have come to detest), but more than forty years as a newspaperman qualifies me to say something about the press that it has not often been willing to assert on its own behalf.

And that is the extraordinarily high degree of personal honesty among its practitioners. I don't believe that the most respected elements in American life — doctors or lawyers — can even approach the incorruptibility of newspapermen.

In my many decades in the business, I have known of only three colleagues who I was reasonably sure were on the take. One was an early city editor, one was a political reporter, and the third was a gossip columnist — all long ago vanished from the profession, to the general scorn of their coworkers.

Yet almost nobody is in a better position to solicit or accept bribes, either for printing puffery about a public figure, or for withholding damaging reports of monkey-business in diverse areas of activity.

Newspaper people know many things they do not print, either because they cannot prove them legally, or because they are shameful revelations of sexual, marital, alcoholic, or other discreditable habits.

If anyone is in a position to blackmail others — and others who are usually able to pay handsomely for silence — it is the reporters or, more rarely, the editors. Such scandals, however, are exceedingly rare, the main reason being that almost nobody enters newspapering in order to make a great deal of money.

As a class, newspapermen are not morally superior to any other group; indeed, some may be quite disreputable, in their personal habits and private lives; but they, on the whole, lack the pecuniary "bump" in their brain that makes wealth or affluence a prime desideratum. This is a goal they willingly leave to their publishers.

What they enjoy most is knowing things, knowing things that the public at large does not know and that should not or cannot be published without violating the canons of decency or the laws of libel. Their professional pleasure lies largely in being "insiders," and they would rather know where the pot of gold is buried, and by whom, than gain possession of any part of it by illicit means.

In these days of so many illegitimate and ignorant attacks upon the press, it may be time to point out that, given the greatest opportunities, newspapermen, who stick their noses into everyone's business, manage far better than most to keep their noses clean.

The only true and useful prophets are not those who predict what is going to happen, but those who warn us of what is most likely to happen unless we do something about it beforehand.

As Language Changes, So Must the Law

ONE OF THE BIG PROBLEMS with what we call law is that so much of it is really a matter of language. In a living language like English, words keep changing their meanings, and what a word meant to lawmakers a generation ago may no longer fit its modern application.

Two matters were taken up by the higher courts this year that pose a real semantic difficulty. For instance, what is a *home*? This sounds simple on its face — but is a "trailer" a home, even though it may be called a "mobile home"?

The police say not; a home is a permanent habitation and requires a warrant in order for police to enter it; a trailer is more like an automobile and may be entered without a warrant if there are reasonable grounds for suspicion.

An allied question pertains to the word *search*. Police cannot conduct a search of someone's body or personal possessions without reasonable grounds — but what about using trained dogs to sniff out possible caches of drugs and other controlled substances?

If the dogs detect such drugs, is it then legal for the police to seize them and turn them over for laboratory analysis? Does the use of animals constitute a violation of privacy if they smell cocaine in a handbag?

I don't pretend to know the answer to either of these thorny questions. What is fascinating is the way in which habits, customs, inventions, and devices outrun the resources of legal language from year to year and decade to decade.

In the beginning of our judicial system, as "common law" was interpreted in Britain, a man was to be judged by "a jury of his peers" — but this meant something quite different from what it does today. If a titled person was accused, the jury in olden times was made of his peers only; that is, from other members of the peerage in the House of Lords.

No others were considered his peers, or equals, in a caste society. As adapted to the new American government, this was dropped, and all qualified citizens were called to jury duty. But then we began to see that this was more fiction than fact, for all-white juries were far more likely to condemn a black defendant than they would a white one.

Now we recognize that a jury should be balanced by color as well as by occupation or rank, to accommodate the realities of race prejudice in this country. And so, "a jury of his peers" has taken on quite a different meaning in 1984, for example, from what it had even a generation earlier.

The law changes far more slowly than anything else in society, and perhaps it is good that it does. But unless we keep re-examining our language, the law will lag too far behind the demands of distributive justice.

The Client's Interest Is Not the Only One

HOW FAR SHOULD AN ATTORNEY GO to advance or protect the interests of his client? How far should a prosecutor go to obtain a conviction that will enhance his record? These are basically ethical questions, rather than legal ones. Most attorneys will not break the law to win a case, but they will bend it, twist it, tie it up in technical knots, or simply fail to exercise scrupulous fairness toward the evidence on the other side.

Many lawyers justify such tactics. They agree with Lord Brougham, who, in a speech at a banquet of the Middle Temple Hall, spoke of "the first great duty of an advocate to reckon everything subordinate to the interests of his client."

But Chief Justice Cockburn of the Queen's Bench, replying to the toast to "the judges of England," said (amid loud cheers from a distinguished assembly of lawyers): "The arms which an advocate wields he ought to use as a warrior, not as an assassin. He ought to uphold the interests of his clients *per fa, non* *per nesfa.** He ought to know how to reconcile the interests of his clients with the eternal interests of truth and justice."

The legal profession should be held in the highest esteem by the citizenry of a country, for the notion of law is one of the noblest man has ever conceived and put into practice. Instead, we find it held in suspicion, if not in contempt, by the bulk of laymen who have come into personal contact with the machinery of the law.

Winning may be everything in a war, and the most important thing in a sport (though even here I disagree), but it surely must take second place to fairness and decency and civility in the courts of justice — or else it becomes a mere tool or weapon for the manipulation of the weak by the strong, the simple by the cunning, and the trusting by the duplicitous.

Words like *truth* and *justice* are cynically laughed at in the corridors of courts, because they are thought to be lovely abstractions that can be neither defined nor reached by mortal men. Yet, they must remain as *goals* — however ultimately unattainable — or the law is shorn of all its dignity and strength and turns into a mere contest of technical prowess and tenacity of purpose.

You can grind an opponent down, you can wear him out in time and money, you can withhold evidence favorable to him, and inflate evidence favorable to yourself — you can do a thousand things in the name of the law, when all you are doing is subverting it to vanity and greed.

In countries like England, self-deprecation is a form of good manners, and is not taken at face value; in America, self-deprecation is more often believed — and lowers one's value in the eyes of others.

* A Ciceronian phrase, meaning "by fair means, not foul."

Crime Increases as Community Declines

IN ALL MY LIFE, I could not recall anything's having been stolen from me; then, suddenly, within a period of weeks, a bag with most of my summer clothes was stolen at the Sarasota airport and my new car was stolen off the street in Chicago.

Both were fully insured, so I suffered more inconvenience than actual loss. But what surprised me was the *insult* I felt to my personal integrity — almost, I could imagine, the way a woman would feel if she were the victim of a rape.

I recognize that theft and duplicity have existed at least as far back as Jacob and Esau, and that nations as well as individuals have always taken what is not theirs by force or by guile. In that sense, we have made no progress in civil relations.

It doesn't seem to matter if a country is rich or poor, united or divided, democratic or despotic — no system in itself seems able to eradicate, or even reduce significantly, the rapacity of our species. Other animals prey because of hunger; we prey mostly for greed.

Yet there does seem to be one limiting factor, and only one, to this "species-specific" trait of man — and that is size. The size of a community bears a direct relation to the incidence of theft and general dishonesty.

Villages and rural communities have always been proud of the fact that, until quite recently, residents could leave their doors unlocked, their cars with the keys dangling in the ignition, and even packages unattended, without the slightest fear of theft.

This was mainly because everyone knew everyone else, and even those with larcenous tendencies were inhibited by this proximity. You simply did not steal from a neighbor or from someone you knew, just as children would not shoplift from a local merchant as casually as they might pilfer from a large chain store.

Conditions have changed, though, even in villages and rural societies. In more recent years, their rate of crimes "against property" have not merely doubled — they have multiplied many times. Not because people have become worse, but because of increased mobility.

People move more than ever; the sense of neighborhood is breaking down; and the omnipresence of the motor vehicle makes it easy for strangers to come and go at will. Cohesiveness is all but lost.

Locks and bolts and alarm systems, and even harsh penalties, will not reduce the incidence of theft. Only a renewed sense of belonging can do this. And we are moving far and fast in the opposite direction.

Defense Is Obsolete in Nuclear Age

ONE OF THE GREAT IMPOSTURES practiced by all nations today is the use of the word *defense* to designate their military apparatus. The fact is that no such thing exists in the modern world. There is only retaliation.

This truth is too slowly creeping into the consciousness of peoples everywhere. We have a Department of Defense, but it cannot defend us; nor can the Russians, nor anyone else, defend themselves against us.

Nations were formed to protect their citizenry, but in the nuclear age no nation is equipped to do this any longer. It can only threaten an equal, or greater, amount of devastation.

War has changed its character radically in the nuclear age — not merely in a quantitative sense, but qualitatively also. It is now simply no less than a mutual suicide pact, each adversary simultaneously holding a loaded pistol to the temple of the other.

Hitherto, all history of warfare has been a seesaw, a catch-up game between weapons of offense and the countervailing weapons of defense. No sooner was a new weapon devised than the means to combat it came into existence.

Now we have reached the end of that perilous road. For the first time in human history, there is no effective defense against warheads. There is only flight — and retaliation.

We have developed the most powerful weaponry the world has ever known and spent more for it than ever before — but we must stop pretending, to ourselves and to others, that it serves the purpose of defense. As long as we keep thinking in these terms, we will be the victims of the most terrible delusion of mankind.

If a nation can no longer protect its civilian population — and no one can doubt that millions would be slaughtered in a nuclear confrontation — then the whole traditional concept of *defense* has been swept off the board.

Even if we accept the best possible scenario, and assume that each of the great powers, such as the United States and the Soviet Union, has too much to lose by a "first strike," as more and more of the smaller nations achieve nuclear capability, the odds mount that one of them will use it — accidentally or crazily or in a fit of desperation. The countries with the least to lose are the ones most to fear in this respect.

Politics is not a rational discipline; if it were, dozens of wars could have been avoided in the past — and in the more recent past, too, as the Falklands conflict should make plain to the objective observer. Power is an irrational element in human affairs, and now, for the first time, we have more power than this fragile globe can sustain.

We have no "enemy" greater than the common enemy, war. And those who prate of "defense" are deluded or dead to reality.

There are two sides to every question — and generally a third side that neither disputant is willing to concede.

Darwin Was No Social Darwinist

READING PETER BRENT'S luminous biography of Charles Darwin, I recalled the remarks attributed both to Sigmund Freud and to Karl Marx. Freud is supposed to have said, "I am not a Freudian," and Marx, "I am not a Marxist."

True or not, what is meant by these ironic disclaimers, of course, is that their followers and interpreters had so distorted or vulgarized their theories that they no longer resembled the original thoughts of the founder. (I suspect that Jesus would have said much the same thing.)

In Darwin's case, the damage has been equally great in the century since he died. The people who called themselves Social Darwinists latched on to the phrase *survival of the fittest* and perverted it to rationalize and justify man's inhumanity to man.

This pained Darwin even beyond the attacks of his enemies, for he expressly stated that the struggle for survival under conditions of "natural selection" resulted from success in *reproducing* the species, not success in enslaving, exploiting, or slaughtering one's fellows.

And the "fittest" species were not necessarily the largest, the strongest, the most aggressive or ferocious, but rather those that best adapted to changing conditions in the environment.

Cooperation, for Darwin, was as much a factor in survival as competition; indeed, there is no species which has evolved by eliminating its weakest members. Killing among animals is limited to the need for food, and "dog eat dog" is a human perversion, for individuals of the same animal species almost never kill, much less consume, their own kind.

Darwin went even further, pointing out that the human invention of war promoted survival of the *unfit*. As he wrote:

The bravest men, who were always willing to come to the front in war, and who freely risked their lives for others, would on the average perish in larger numbers than other men. . . . In every country in which a standing army is kept up, the fairest young men are taken . . . and thus exposed to early death during war . . . while the feebler are left at home and have a much better chance to propagate their kind.

Actually, it is man's intelligence, not natural selection, that has given us everything we call culture and civilization. By intelligence we have removed ourselves from the domination of the biological process, so that man is in large part the master of his own evolution.

What we call aggression in man is quite different from that in other species; with them, it is a blind instinct; with us it is a power drive that threatens to exterminate our species. The salient fact about the Social Darwinists is that they are antisocial.

There seems little point in advising a man without shoes to raise himself by his own bootstraps.

■

No program or set of proposals I have ever looked at closely has been as bad as its critics insisted, or as sound as its proponents have claimed.

■

Economics without ethics is exploitation; ethics without economics is rhetoric.

■

When a potentially dangerous drug like cocaine turns into a "status symbol," we are desperately in need of new status symbols that will enhance life, not threaten it.

It is far more important for a society to have a floor under income than a ceiling over it, and a "negative" income tax to assure this is more important than a system to prevent people from going through the ceiling.

■

The poor magnify the opulence of the rich, and the rich minimize the squalor of the poor.

■

There is no effective "solution" to the drug problem as long as there is an effective demand for narcotics; the most we can hope for is a rational formula that will optimize the deterrence of the American system with the flexibility of the British system of drug control.

■

The contestant who understands the rules will always win, except when he comes up against one who understands the exceptions to those rules.

■

No matter what time of year it is, if you are in Florida you will get sweet corn that has been frozen and shipped down from Michigan; if you are in Michigan, you will get sweet corn that has been frozen and shipped up from Florida.

■

Before any law is passed, the legislative body would do well to ponder the old Roman maxim that it is a hundred times easier to enact a statute than to get rid of it.

■

I would be inclined to invest in any corporation whose annual report included the frank notation: "Goofs We Made Last Year."

PART II

OF THE
LIFE OF THE SPIRIT

Learning to Live with Ambiguity

IN A QUESTION PERIOD following a lecture, one of the college students in the audience asked, "What is the most important lesson you've learned in life?"

I had no hesitancy in replying, "How to accept ambiguity and live with it."

What I meant was learning how not to be frozen into one attitude toward events that happen in the world, to myself or to others.

Human life is many things, both wonderful and terrible. It is a mixed fabric of good and evil, happiness and horror, matters we can control to some degree and matters beyond our control.

We can do much, but not all; the task is to do as much as we can and to accept what comes after that — to acknowledge both the efforts of free will, and the ultimate decisions of fate.

Ambiguity is the very essence of human existence. Almost nobody is loved as much as he or she would like to be; nobody succeeds in every area of life, just as nearly nobody fails in every area. We cannot change the cards we were dealt; we can only play the hand to the best.

People who cannot or will not accept ambiguity in the human condition are the most miserable and disappointed of all. They are either swimming upstream or sinking, drowning, when they can float.

Most people today fail to recognize that happiness is a fairly recent aspiration of the human race. For most of history, survival was the goal — coping, making do, struggling against the caprices of natural disasters and the blows of social and economic injustice.

The acceptance of ambiguity implies more than the commonplace understanding that some good things and some bad things happen to us. It means that we know that good and evil are inextricably intermixed in human affairs; that they contain, and sometimes embrace, their opposites; that success may involve failure of a different kind, and failure may be a kind of triumph.

"The test of a first-rate intelligence," wrote F. Scott Fitzgerald, "is the ability to hold two opposed ideas in the mind at the same time, and still function." Few temperaments, much less minds, are able to do this.

We must learn to extract the sweet and endure the bitter, often from the same potion. The dice are loaded — but only in the sense that it takes us so long to absorb the elementary lesson that it may be too late to benefit from it in time.

And it is the basic ambiguity of life that prompted Aristotle to say that no man can know whether he is happy or not until it is time for him to die.

God's House Has Many Rooms

As I sat in a coffee shop near the window one day, watching the stream of humanity passing along the street, I was struck again with the incredible diversity of our species.

We are all so amazingly and wonderfully individual, not only in looks but in every other way, unlike other species, that there must be some deep reason for it. Even identical twins do not have identical fingerprints.

Why, then, when our Creator has been so profligate and painstaking to produce so many unique specimens, should we expect that He demands all of us to worship in the same way? He could have made all of us one color, or one height, or one uniform configuration.

"In my Father's house are many rooms," said Rabbi Jesus, and it is reasonable to assume that what was meant by this is that there are rooms for pygmies and giants, for Christians and Buddhists, and even for believers and nonbelievers.

Almost all people who designate themselves as "religious" are exclusivists; that is, they think there is only one road to heaven, and that path means to share in their particular faith.

To me, this is a denigration of God, not a glorification; it is pulling Him down to the human level, rather than accepting and exulting in the diversity and multiplicity of His works.

I once suggested in a column that "nobody has a pipeline to God," and the next mail brought a flood of letters pointing to the Bible. But five hundred million Chinese never heard of the Bible, and hundreds of millions of other humans are likewise ignorant of it.

It is hard for me to believe that a special "revelation" would be granted to a small number of Jews in a tiny land, and again to an even smaller number of early Christians (all of them also Jews) in the same place, while ignoring the masses of Africa, Asia, Europe, and the rest of the globe.

This is not the way divinity works, in my opinion. There are too many different kinds of people in the world, worshiping in diverse ways, for any tribe or sect to be given exclusive rights to disseminate the Word — and to promote it by bloodshed more than by love.

The "many rooms" in the house means there is room for all humans who are upright and wish well for their fellows. My God does not even require to be "adored." He is quite content to be "followed," which is much harder than bowing, praying, preaching, or "converting." The Kingdom of Heaven is far more spacious than the exclusivists imagine.

"Religions" in Name Only

IT MAY BE well worth the price, but one of the real perils that cannot be overlooked in America's "separation of church and state" is the formation of many "religions" in name only.

The government cannot and will not interfere with a legally established nonprofit "church," and almost anyone can set up such an institution, for personal gain or power or both, without worrying too much about its integrity.

It can call itself a "Church of God" or a "Church of Christ," or "Spiritual Rejuvenation Church," or anything like that, and provide its leaders with a fleet of Rolls-Royces and millions in property investments, and preach the most deceptive or diabolic of creeds.

You can be a faker of the worst kind, or the most malignant hater, or a con man of transparent duplicity — but as long as you maintain the proper façade, you can amass a fortune for personal glory and for propagandizing the rest of the gullible public.

Some of what we now call "sects" are honest and honorable; others are merely shields from income taxation and deeper scrutiny. But, given our constitutional guarantees, the latter are as protected as the former from investigation and assessment.

While freedom of religion — which includes, of course, freedom *from* religion — is an integral part of our system, at the same time it permits, and may even encourage, the formation and growth of social and political causes masquerading as solely religious enterprises.

There seems to be no fair or easy solution to this pernicious state of affairs. Government must maintain a hands-off policy, except where actual fraud can be shown; on the other hand, if anyone is permitted to start a so-called church, the most vicious or corrupt of demagogues can freely peddle their wares in the religious market.

One wonders whether religious education of a sort should be required in the nation's high schools and colleges — not as dogma or faith, but historically and philosophically, so that the emergent generations obtain a clearer understanding of what churches mean and how they can be used to pervert their basic spiritual commitment.

We are one of the most ignorant countries in the world on this delicate, and often decisive, subject. Only an informed public is equipped to discriminate between a palpable fraud and a genuine expression of reverence. It would be a ticklish task, but anything less leaves our children vulnerable to the beguilements of intolerance, bigotry, and emotional manipulation by evilly self-appointed messiahs.

Four-Letter Words Are Not a Moral Issue

PASSING ACROSS MY DESK recently was a "Report on Profanity," issued by a so-called watchdog outfit named the Coalition for Better Television. The report said, in effect, that "nasty words" were up 140 percent over last year, in some thirteen hundred hours of prime-time TV it had monitored.

The most frequently used four-letter words on television, it disclosed, are *hell* and *damn*. But how insensitive to language can you get? *Hell* and *damn,* in the vocabulary of today, are not *profanity* — they are merely punctuation marks.

"Where the hell did I put my shoes?" and "That damn dog is barking again" have absolutely nothing to do with the theological concepts of eternal punishment or salvation; they have no meaning except as emotional emphasis.

The widespread use of these words in ordinary conversation has about as much significance as an exclamation mark. They have become as secular and inoffensive as *heck* and *darn,* which are now too weak to express genuine exasperation or annoyance.

What is wrong with these words is not moral, but esthetic; they impoverish language, just as the obscene four-letter words do, by filling emotive gaps with meaningless syllables.

What a waste of time and effort to monitor television for such inconsequential nonsense, when it is the very *substance* of the programming, not the form, that is so demeaning to the human mind and spirit.

A sensible Coalition for Better Television would focus its energy and influence on trying to raise the public's standard of viewing more than rebuking the broadcasters' standard of programming. As long as the public is more than willing to tolerate inane sitcoms and the mindless violence of adventure serials, the networks will keep offering this commercially rewarding pap.

Nobody was ever hurt by four-letter words: Shakespeare, indeed, is full of the most outrageously obscene language, even in one of his greatest plays, *Hamlet*. But he was a highly moral writer, in the deepest sense of his values and his portrayals of character and conduct. If anyone ever knew right from wrong, it was he.

Too many self-appointed guardians of "morals" tend to concentrate on the superficial and the irrelevant, while ignoring the basic infrastructure of the spiritual life. This was precisely the charge that Jesus laid against the priests and preachers of his own day — and little has changed since then, except that those he railed against now call themselves his followers.

No doubt there is a "higher law" — but it will be respected only in a higher place.

■

The fiercest people are not those who are bold, but those who are frightened.

Beware the Bible Quoters

THE MOST TIRESOME LETTERS I receive come from the Bible-quoters. Whenever I express an opinion that does not fit into their snug little doctrine, they advise me to consult Matthew 2:12 or Thessalonians 9:6 or the whole Book of Daniel.

It has been my experience, however, that there is almost an inverse ratio between "reading" the Bible and trying to understand it. The most frequent quoters seem to have the least comprehension of the way that the Gospel was composed and compiled.

They look upon it as "the Word of God," and in a sense it may be. But not in the sense they imagine. This Word was filtered through the minds and hearts of men, and during the hundreds of years it took shape on paper, it became only a smudged carbon copy of the original.

As a historical and metaphysical and literary anthology of religious beliefs, it is a curious patchwork of fact and fiction, wisdom and superstition, myth and poetry, hopes and dreams, prophecies and fantasies.

You have to know *how* to read it, or it is worse than useless; it is a dangerous book for the ignorant, the bigoted, the deluded, and the self-justifying — which all of us are, to some extent.

You can find almost anything you want in the Old and New Testaments: you can justify witchcraft and the burning of heretics and apostates; you can defend slavery and the domination of women and the sacrifice of children.

You can also find the most magnificent appeals to love and mercy and justice and brotherhood; the most laudable condemnations of war and nationalism and hardness of heart and coldness of mind. Almost everything is there, if you know how to select it and where to find it.

The Bible-quoters, of course, select only those passages that seem to validate their, or their church's, dogmas. They are supremely unaware of Biblical scholarship, among both the Protestants and the Catholics, that carefully analyzes and separates the different strands and distinguishes fable and metaphor from fact and history.

Reading the Bible without such intellectual equipment is like walking through a minefield without a detector. Faith is a fine thing to have, but only after you have gone as far as reason will take you. If you stop short, you are doing a disservice to God, Who provided man with reason in His own image.

Please, no more letters citing the Gospel. If you treat every word in it as Gospel, you are betraying God's greatest gift.

As Knowledge Grows, Religion Should Change

I HAVE NEVER BEEN ABLE TO UNDERSTAND the presupposition that the only subject in the world that isn't supposed to change is religion. Everything else we know, or think we know, is subject to alteration and modification as we learn more about it.

Only religion seems to be frozen in its sources of thousands of years ago, even though our whole picture of the universe has changed radically in every aspect, from the tiny electron to the vast galaxy.

What we loosely call "God" may be eternal and changeless, but our perceptions of the ultimate reality are far different now from the "three-storied" universe of ancient and medieval times. Along with this, the view of man's place in the world has undergone a drastic transformation.

Religions should grow as our knowledge and understanding grow. Our idea of God cannot remain a static one if we believe we have been given the gift of reason and were created in the image of His thought. Our capacity to learn more about ourselves and the cosmos is the imprint of divinity that marks us off from the rest of the animal world. To reject our new knowledge out of hand is surely to worship a false idol.

It is interesting that fundamentalists of all religions — whether Christian, Jewish, or Moslem — are more alike than they are different. Whatever their doctrinal divisions (which they hold to so fiercely), they all share a common perspective: *Do not question, look backward, believe in the Word, and discard nothing of the past.*

But man is a creature designed expressly to ask questions, to look forward, to interpret the Word, and to discard what is no longer believable or usable in the light of examination and testing. Life is dynamic, not static, and while our ultimate concerns may not change, our approach to them must and should.

In fact, God Himself changed in the Old Testament alone — from a tribal deity to a universal one, as the prophets broadened and deepened the notion of divinity; and changed once more, when the early Jewish Christians expanded worship from the Law to the Person.

All formal religion is still too parochial, too narrow, too rigid, too divisive and contentious, to represent the reality of a cosmos beyond our conception. It is still too wedded to myths that are useful only as symbols and are dangerous if taken as literal portraits of the way the world was made and made to run.

A faith based on stubborn ignorance cannot be what God wants of us.

Two thousand years after the founding of Christianity, the only people who habitually turn the other cheek are photographic models.

■

Why do so many people pray to acquire good fortune, and so few pray to acquire good judgment?

"Christian" Church Drove Blacks to Islam

IT SEEMS PROBABLE TO ME that if I had been born black in America, and especially in a black urban ghetto, I would have become a Moslem rather than a Christian — by conversion, as so many blacks have.

It is not that Islam is superior to Christianity as a religion (all religions, in my view, fail to live up to their founders' hopes), but that white Christianity consistently rejected its black brothers while recognizing no color bar.

It was not always thus: In centuries past, the Arab countries were avid slave-traders and did as much as anybody else to capture, sell, and transport slaves. But Islam learned the error of its ways, while Christendom perpetuated the isolation and exploitation of blacks, particularly in our presumably "democratic" nation.

The great pity of it was that, in the beginning, our black population was among the most fervent segment of church-going, Bible-believing, Jesus-inspired congregations in the country. More than any other, they were filled with faith and hope — but they experienced little charity from their white brothers.

Like most rejected suitors, in gradual but mounting disappointment, the blacks sought another faith that might deliver what the missionaries had only promised and not delivered — and, in the modern world, Islam seemed to offer the greatest opportunity to common worship on an equal basis.

"If you won't fully accept us, we'll find some church that will" was the implicit attitude of many blacks. "There has to be some universal religion that practices what it preaches, here and now."

This has been one of the greatest failures of Christendom, and one of the most blasphemous betrayals of the Gospel of Jesus. These people, taken forcibly from their homes, were deliberately treated like oxen and denied the status of ordinary humanity.

Despite this denigration, they embraced the Christian tenets and kept waiting for them to be actualized in everyday life. Generations passed, and only token gestures were made in their direction by their white co-religionists.

I am surprised they had the patience to wait so long before disillusionment set in. When it did, the reaction was predictable — thousands of the brightest and the best (and the bitterest) turned from the cross to the crescent. And they will not be easily wooed back by sermons in syrup.

Golden Rule Stops Short

IF YOU THINK ABOUT IT long and deeply enough, you will see that the so-called Golden Rule is only gold-plated. It is useful and beneficent in limited contexts, but it fails to go far enough. As the social scientists would say, it is "culture-bound."

"Do unto others as you would have them do unto you" is not the exclusive possession of Western religion, as many suppose it is. The Eastern religions of the world embody much the same precept; in Buddhism, indeed, it is expressed with rather more subtlety and sensitivity in its negative form: "Do not do unto others what you would not have them do unto you."

The trouble with the Golden Rule is that it starts from where *you* are, rather than from where the other person is. It assumes that the other person wants whatever you want and that what you want is right for him as well. This ethnocentric attitude was used to justify the forced "conversion" of infidels to Christians — since I wanted to go to heaven and felt sure that the only vehicle was my religion, I was really doing a favor to the heathens by converting them to my beliefs.

The Golden Rule does not admit of a plurality of cultures; it wants to press everyone into the same mold — and the mold is our mold. Inestimable damage has been done to native peoples, using this imperialistic notion, and rationalizing it as being "for their own good," as if we knew better than they what their own good really was.

A far more sensible version would be: "Do unto others as they would have you do unto them." This attitude requires, not the sentimental arrogance of assuming that you know what is best for them, but respect for and understanding of your cultural differences — what the Germans untranslatably call your *weltanshauung*.

The Golden Rule may have been suitable in the ancient world, when little or nothing was known of diverse cultures, when China and the Far East might have been in another universe, when the existence of the Americas was not even suspected, when all of civilization as then known was contained in the Mediterranean basin or nearby. It certainly represented an ethical step forward from earlier codes of conduct. But it was meant to be a steppingstone, not a stoppingplace. It signaled an advance in human thinking and empathizing, rather than a dead end, an eternal precept requiring no further examination or revision. The New Testament expanded on the Old as a *further* revelation, not necessarily as a *final* one.

In modern society, the Golden Rule needs to be amended to recognize the diversity of cultures and the right of each culture to pursue its own ways (so long as it does not infringe upon another culture), just as we respect the right of the individual to be his or her own person. All we have the right to ask of others is civility; when we demand uniformity we are tarnishing the Golden Rule beyond recognition.

It may be hard for many people to say "I was wrong," but it is even harder for the self-righteous to forgive them.

Real Achievements Lie in the Present

THE HIGHEST AND PERHAPS MOST PERVASIVE of human vanities is the desire to have our names — and our works — remembered for as long as possible. We like to feel that a part of us, at least, will be recalled and well regarded in the ages to come. But what we forget, or do not care to note, is that when you die, you are dead forever, at least in sublunary terms. And forever is a time beyond grasping — billions of years, unto infinity. What we call "civilization" today will utterly crumble into dust, as fully as Ninevah or Tyre.

Even Horace's monuments — those constructed of verse — will be just as lost in time as the brass and gold he scorned. English, no less than Latin, will be an extinct language, nearly indecipherable, found among the rubble, excavated only by a few fanatical scholars and archeologists.

"Vanity, vanity, all is vanity," wrote the Preacher in the Book of Ecclesiastes, and we do not know his name or who he was. All our efforts to attain immortality — by statesmanship, by conquest, by science or the arts — are equally vain in the long run, because the long run is longer than any of us can imagine. *Eternity* is a term that eludes both the intelligence and the imagination of man.

If this be true, where does our real achievement lie? It lies only in the present, in who we are now, in what we do, in how we relate to the persons and problems around us, in the living world. This is the real meaning and message of religion, not the angels and the harps and the pearly gates and all the rest of that popular mythology. Whether we are dead forever, or "return" in some form we cannot comprehend, the only real future we have is now, the only acts that matter are here, the only goodness we can perform is with and among and toward our fellows.

Jesus never asked to be worshiped or adored. He asked only to be followed — among the poor, the sick, the despised, the outcasts, the tax-collectors who were loathed and the prostitutes who were rejected. It is too hard for most people to follow him so they ensconce him in "heaven" instead, substituting piety for imitation and seeking escape from the commandments by selecting only that part of his message they find congenial to their tastes and inclinations.

There is only one way to have reverence, no matter what your creed. And that is to love even when you do not like, to give even when you would rather take, to lose yourself in eternity by finding yourself in time. Whether immortality or nothing awaits us at the end, religion is but a hollowness and a mask unless we become what we are meant to be in the present moment.

What Belongs to Caesar, and What to God?

IN AN ESSAY discussing the letters it received from readers during the previous year, *Time* magazine disclosed that its cover story dealing with the Roman Catholic bishops' stand against nuclear war elicited an unusually broad response, both pro and con.

What I found most interesting was that many of the "con" letters quoted the Bible to the bishops: *"Render unto Caesar the things which are Caesar's, and unto God the things that are God's."*

These correspondents wrongly suppose that Jesus is making a statement or giving an answer, when he is really asking a question. As Father John McKenzie, author of the learned *Dictionary of the Bible,* puts it: "His words tell the questioners to answer their own question."

What are the things that properly belong to Caesar? And which are the ones that belong to God? These are matters we are called on to work out for ourselves.

If we let Caesar decide which things belong to him, he will claim everything, up to and including our lives and souls. All that Jesus conceded in that passage was that the coin had a portrait of Caesar on it, and therefore currency belongs to the state. But does human life?

And this is precisely what I mean when I suggest that the Bible cannot be consulted as a book of answers, but as a book that puts the basic questions to us at an existential level. We reply to these questions in the way our background, our conditioning, and our intellectual freedom call for.

Each contesting and conflicting sect can find the answers it wants, by reading them into the text. Slavery was long justified by quoting the Bible; fratricide was condoned; the subjugation of women was accepted as "God's law." Tyrants, most of all, have used the Bible to keep their populace enchained and their hereditary privileges intact.

Just how much should we render unto Caesar is the real question. Should we follow our state into nuclear war? Is that our patriotic duty, or a violation of God's higher law? These are matters that each of us has to decide for himself, after paying close attention to the bishops and to the warriors, both hot and cold. The answers are not "given."

Much can be learned from the Bible, as a repository of wisdom — but its lessons must be understood and digested and reflected upon with an honest heart and a clear mind. It is not like an ancient oracle dispensing absolute answers, but a living presence requiring us to respond to moral problems that have confronted mankind, in different ways, since the beginning of history.

If a human life "belongs to God," and even the mother has no right to abort her fetus, then what right does the state possess to take the life of a convicted criminal on the grounds of punishment?

Secret of Life Is Beyond
the Reach of Science

IT IS FOOLISH TO ATTACK SCIENCE, and only ignorant people do so. But it is equally important to distinguish between *science* and *scientism* just as we must distinguish between *religion* and *religiosity*.

Scientific methodology is an absolute must for the human race, to be respected and even venerated. It is the way we learn to separate and combine, which is the essence of intelligence. The greatest advances of the human race have been, and will be, made by this methodology. It is humble, tentative, and perpetually self-correcting.

Scientism is another matter altogether. It is a reductionist activity, in which life is seen as "nothing but" an assortment or collection of material substances operating according to "laws" or "functions" that have no meaning beyond themselves.

Most scientists, regrettably, worship at the shrine of this false idol. While their techniques may be humble, their assumptions are proud: the primary one being that the secret of life may be found in the physical elements of the universe.

Not all of them, however, by any means. One of the most brilliant, the Nobel laureate, Albert Szent-Györgyi, had this to say about the elusive nature of life vis-à-vis science:

In my hunt for the secret of life, I started my research in histology. Unsatisfied by the information that cellular morphology could give me about life, I turned to physiology. Finding physiology too complex, I took up pharmacology. Still finding the situation too complicated, I turned to bacteriology. But bacteria were even too complex, so I descended to the molecular level, studying physical chemistry.

After 20 years' work, I was led to conclude that to understand life we have to descend to the electronic level, and to the world of wave mechanics. But electrons are just electrons and have no life at all. Evidently on the way I lost life; it had run out between my fingers.

"It had run out between my fingers." Exactly. This is the most honest appraisal of what happens in scientific research that seeks to tap the essence of life. If you go down far enough, you come to a dead end; somehow along the way the life process has escaped scrutiny.

It is much like taking apart a watch to see what makes it run: No part can tell you, for it is in the *organization* of parts that the function resides. Science is analytic, but life is holistic — that is, the whole is greater than the simple sum of the parts. Such knowledge is the beginning of wisdom.

Return "Sin" to Its Original Meaning

CERTAIN WORDS, like people, get old and tired and lose their vitality and impact. When they do, they should be retired from active use. My prime candidate for this verbal retirement is the word *sin.*

Not the idea, mind you. I firmly believe there is such a thing as sin, as distinguished from crime, and we are all guilty of it in differing degrees. (Whether it is "original" or not, I will leave to the contesting theologians.)

But the word itself, as it is commonly used, has become so debased, distorted, and abused (mostly by fervently "religious" folk) that it carries little emotional or intellectual force — especially to those to whom it is mostly directed. It has become almost a joke word to skeptics and unbelievers.

It would help, I think, if we returned to the original meaning of the word in Hebrew. To *sin,* in the Old Testament, is literally "to miss the mark." It is to aim at the wrong place, to shoot at the wrong target rather than the proper one for man.

"Sinning" is basically a form of idolatry: It is to make one's goal in life the worship of a false god — not the god of goodness and justice, but the goal of ambition and appetite, of power and domination, of vanity and vindictiveness.

In past ages, as we know, all kinds of trivial and harmless pursuits were labeled and condemned as sins — dancing, playing cards, even enjoying a ball game or picnic on the Sabbath. Each sect had its own canon of sins, and most of the clergy, regrettably, took these more seriously than the most basic sin of all, which is hardness of heart.

When modern man brushed away, or laughed off, these arbitrary and puritanical prohibitions (which really had little or nothing to do with the existential nature of worship), he threw out the baby with the bathwater, and began to regard the whole idea of sin as a figment of primitive imagination, along with the white-robed angels in "heaven" and the pitchfork-wielding imps in "hell."

It might be justly said, indeed, that the rejection of the idea of sin was evoked more by religious zealots than by unbelievers. If you make everything pleasant a sin, you have simply undercut the gravity of the word and trivialized it out of credibility.

Instead of the narrow moralistic meaning it has acquired, *sinning* needs to be restored to its basic metaphor of "missing the mark," of aiming for the wrong circles on the target, of substituting a lesser goal for the bull's eye. We could do with fewer of God's loose-lipped moralists and more of His sharp-eyed marksmen.

Persons, like metals, have different "tensile strengths," and success under pressure only signifies a person's strength, not his essential value — for many go under who have every worthwhile attribute — except toughness.

Words Have No Absolute Meanings

"THERE IS NOT A SENTENCE which adequately states its own meaning," observed Alfred North Whitehead in one of his brilliant essays on science and philosophy. "In fact," he went on, "there is not a sentence, or a word, with a meaning which is independent of the circumstances under which it is uttered."

If you wonder what he meant by this, consider something as simple and definite as a specific sum of money — say $100. To a poor and hungry man in the city, it is a lifesaver, buying more food than he can eat. To a thirsty man in the desert, it is not worth a dime; he would gladly trade it for a cup of water.

Suppose you were handed a $100 bill. The first one could mean a lot. Now suppose you are being handed $100 bills every hour on the hour. By the end of the first day, does the hundred you receive "mean" as much as the first one you got? And what about the end of the first week, or the first month? The longer it goes on, the less the value of each sum; if it goes on long enough, you could light a cigar with a $100 bill, and that would have no more meaning than using a match.

If something seemingly as concrete as a sum of money does not adequately express its own meaning but depends on conditions and circumstances, how much more inadequate are all the abstractions we use daily without even thinking of them — words like *authority* and *liberty* and *equality* and *eternity* and *matter* and *spirit* and *justice* and *law*.

Outside of its context in social reality, no word (except perhaps connectives like *and* and *but*) has an absolute meaning. Unless we understand the "aura" of significance that the word has for its speaker, we cannot really communicate on the same channel and may be using the same common word to talk about two different concepts.

We know that *democracy* implies one thing to the Russians and another to Americans; that *terrorists* and *freedom fighters* depend on where you stand; that my *concerned citizen* may be your *bleeding heart*.

When the early Christians were persecuted by the Romans, it was on the charge that they were "atheists" — because, to the polytheistic Romans, believing only in one god was next to believing in none! For the meaning of a word consists in how we feel about it, and not in its dictionary definition.

Thoughts for a Last Column

"IF YOU KNEW you were going to write your last column," asked a friend yesterday, "what would you choose to say?"

"It has all been said before," I replied, "but since nobody really listens, it has to keep being said over and over again.

"First, that you gain your life by giving it away. This is the hardest and longest lesson to learn, and most of us never learn it or believe it. In the end, we possess nothing except what we have shared or given away. People come to realize this when they make out their wills — but then it is too late, for you are making others happier after your death than in your lifetime.

"Second, that *being* and *becoming* are the proper ends of a human life, and *having* is only a means. Most of us turn the means into an end and never realize the end. And so there is no growth, no change, no development, and we leave the world as we found it, if not worse.

"Third, that we are all part of the great chain of life, and we must forge stronger links, not break them. This means not only with other persons, but with all living things and the forces of nature as well.

"If mankind was given dominion over the Earth, as the Bible tells us, it was not for exploitation, but for stewardship, because we have been endowed with more sense (if not senses) than the other creatures.

"What I would say, finally, is that none of us lives up to the best part of us; we all betray our humanity daily, in dozens of ways, large and small. And this is the ultimate betrayal, because the whole world has been put into our hands, and now we possess the power to destroy it utterly and perhaps permanently.

"Nietzsche described man as a creature who must surpass himself or perish. His 'Superman,' properly understood, is not someone superlative in strength or dominion, but someone who is, in Nietzsche's words, 'an arrow of longing for the other shore.' The other shore is the world as we picture it in our dreams and hopes — a place of concern and comfort and mutual aid, not of ruthless egotism.

"Mankind distorts and perverts whatever is handed to us: We turn the virtue of loyalty into sectarianism, the virtue of courage into murder, the virtue of intelligence into brute domination, the virtue of prudence into greed, the virtue of religion into bigotry, prejudice, and hate. Our awesome record of achievement is equaled, or exceeded, only by our dreadful record of destruction and disintegration. If our planet is eventually destroyed, it will not be the result of natural causes, but by our own free will, choosing the worse in preference to the better. The choice is ours — let us not blame it on anything else."

What we call "individualism" is the most creative of human drives if it is directed toward the fullest development of a person's innate capacities; but it is the most destructive of human drives if it is directed toward supremacy at the expense of others' full development.

■

People eventually reject lies, but they embrace myths; and myths are a hundred times more dangerous than lies.

Fundamentalists Confuse Friends and Foes

NOTHING IS MORE FOOLISH than failing to know your friends from your enemies, or confusing the two. And this is exactly what the fundamentalists do when they attack the "humanists."

Humanists come in all sorts and shapes. Some are atheists. Some are agnostics. Some are believers, like Jacques Maritain, the great Catholic philosopher, who wrote a book defining and defending "Christian humanism." But whatever their shade of religious belief, the humanists are on the side of the angels, even when they do not believe in angels. Their ethical values are high and they have nothing but good will for the human race.

Western theology — whether Christian, Jewish, or Muslim — is based on two strands: love of God and love of our fellow man. Only a saint can combine the two in the highest proportion. The fundamentalists emphasize the love of God. The humanists emphasize the love of man. The real enemies of both are those who are not activated by love but by hate, by envy, by feelings of exploitation or revenge or the disvaluation of all values, both human and divine. It is the anti-humanists who create most of the mischief in society.

Far more threatening than the atheist in the modern world is the person who does not believe in man any more than in God; whose ethical system is warped by love of self (or by hatred of self, which, strangely enough, often comes to the same thing). The only law he pays allegiance to is the law of the jungle; he is not up to the level of being a humanist, much less a lover of God.

If the world is divided at all, it is not between fundamentalists and humanists, but between those who look beyond themselves and those who do not. The ally of the Baptist is not just another Baptist, or a Methodist, or a Jew or a Moslem; it is also all those millions who proclaim the brotherhood of man even though they cannot accept the fatherhood of God. The common enemy is the nihilist, the egotist, the cynic who places himself first and all the others nowhere. I don't think God cares much if we believe in Him as long as we display love of our fellow man; and I don't think He cares much for those who profess to believe in Him and use that belief to bludgeon people who do not share it.

Fundamentalists are stupid to attack humanism when there are so many other things worthy of opposing; and especially since humanism has its ethical roots in the world's great religions, East and West, whether it knows it or not. But, then, if they weren't stupid they might not be so adamantly fundamentalist.

Life Is a Precious Gift

I WAS CHATTING with a friend of one of my sons — a young man not much past thirty — when he said a most extraordinary thing. We were discussing the dozen victims who perished in a recent bridge collapse, when he remarked with all evidence of sincerity, "If I died tomorrow, I would feel I was ahead of the game."

"You would?" I replied with incredulity. "I really would," he insisted. "I've enjoyed my life, done a lot of things, and met a lot of people, and I'm grateful for the experience."

The young man is not what used to be called a "Christer." He was not speaking out of any religious conviction or spiritual assurance. He was simply expressing a personal point of view: an acceptance of the contingency of death with the same equanimity that he accepts and appreciates the gift of life.

And I thought of all the people I know in their fifties and sixties and beyond, who are anxious and resentful and sometimes terrified when illness, or even enervation, gives them an oppressive sense of their mortality.

I myself am not exempt from this feeling. A sudden illness early this spring depressed me more than it should have, when I compare it with some of the ailments that afflict my contemporaries, and even persons much younger than I.

And how much more have I to be grateful for than that young man. I have lived twice as long, done more, seen more, learned more, tasted more pleasures, and satisfied more goals. If we can make a calculus of contributions to the permanent heritage of the human race, why should I expect, or feel I deserve, a lengthier life than Mozart and Beethoven, Shakespeare and Montaigne, Lincoln and Thoreau, Raphael and Rembrandt, and scores of others whose lives were cut short by one cause or another?

We forget too easily that life is exactly that — a gift, or, if you will, a happy accident. It calls for no merit on our part, and every day we live is a bonus denied to thousands by the wheel of fortune — like the dozen workmen struck down without warning on the fatal bridge.

This may not be, as Leibnitz asserted (and as Voltaire satirized) the best of all possible worlds; but it is the only world we know for certain, and the spermatozoic odds were at least a million to one against our knowing it at all.

It is hard to believe, especially when young, that we are going to die; but it is this certain knowledge that accounts for what Tillich calls our "ontic anxiety." No other creature on earth has been instilled with this awareness of eventual death, and this is our burden. The way to lighten it is to reflect that being here at all is an adventure that none of us would have wished to miss, even though it ends on a dying note.

Continued good health attunes us to the external world but distances us from our internal selves; it is illness that tells us what we really are.

Catastrophes Bring Out the Best in People

OF COURSE, all those plagues and pestilences and floods we read about in the Old Testament were not the "hand of God" reaching down to exact retribution for man's misdeeds, but we must ask ourselves why natural disasters play such a prominent part in Scriptural history.

My own answer, at least, is that the wise men who wrote the book were showing us something about human conduct and the human condition, which is still relevant today.

What we see during natural disasters is the best part of us responding to the worst conditions. People become genuine neighbors overnight, helping each other to a heroic extent. Faced with a common adversary — the elements — men, women, and children forget their ordinary divisions and act for their mutual preservation and support.

Even thousands of those not threatened by floods, for example, promptly pitch in and offer aid and housing to those desolated by these freaks of nature. There is no time or energy left for the customary incivilities of life.

When these same phenomena took place in ancient times, no doubt the credulous and the superstitious attributed them to God's displeasure. Whether the learned scribes who wrote the Bible also did so is a matter of speculation. What I think is truer to suggest is that they used these devices as symbolism to bring home the lesson both of man's unity and of his relative impotence in the face of such batterings.

The Bible is replete with warnings of this kind, showing how frail a reed is man compared with the elemental forces. By dramatic parable, it tells us that the fatherhood of God implies the brotherhood of man. If it were written at the end of the twentieth century, it would use nuclear fission and acid rain and dioxide poisoning instead of the primitive examples it provides.

People are what they are meant to be only when they become more than they normally are; only when they are bound together in fear and comradeship. Then the accretions of the ego drop away, and they recognize that their primordial loyalty is to one another. But, alas, as soon as the emergency is over, they revert to their prior selves, forgetting the lesson, as children do when school is out.

It may take a global catastrophe — whether nature-made or man-made — to bring us to our senses, to convince us that we have been alienated from ourselves during the long course of human history.

No One Has a Pipeline to God

YOU MAY HAVE HEARD THE STORY of the little boy in art class who was busy at work when the teacher came up behind him and asked, "What are you doing?"

"I'm drawing a picture of God," the little boy replied.

"But nobody knows what God looks like," protested the teacher.

"Well," said the little boy, "they will when I get through."

Most of those fervent preachers on the Sunday morning television programs remind me of this little boy — but whereas he didn't know any better, they should.

For a combination of arrogance and ignorance (which they mistakenly interpret as "faith"), it is hard to beat these clergymen. St. Thomas, the greatest theologian of the Middle Ages, admitted that we cannot know what God *is,* only what He is *not* — but these spellbinders insist that they know how He wants us to vote.

To me, at least, the greatest blasphemy in the world is not the denial of God's existence, but the claim that we have a pipeline to Him, and that all the other claimants are wrong. This assertion is what plunged the world into the bloodiest of wars in the past, and might well do so again if the zealots had their way.

If there is a Supreme Plan for mankind, it is surely beyond our comprehension. You can quote the Bible nine ways to Sunday, and each sect will come up with a different version of God's Will. I don't happen to believe that He would have revealed the truth to some and not to others. A God who plays favorites is not my idea of deity.

The concept of God is still evolving in the human mind, and is far from finished. It changes as we learn more about the universe and about ourselves. Monotheism was a great advance over animism and polytheism, but the Jehovah of the Old Testament and the Jesus of the New are only steps upward on the road of human comprehension.

There is still far more that we do not know than we know. As science progresses, we find creation more mysterious, not less. This should instill in us more reverence for the workings of the cosmos, and less cockiness about what God has seen fit to reveal to us.

We cannot know, we can only guess at, ultimate answers, and no religion can do more than contemplate the infinite from its own particular perspective in history. Each of them, I am sure, would be equally astounded at the amount of error compounded with the elements of truth in its doctrines.

Only God knows what the answer is, and He is only hinting, not telling, no matter what is preached on Sunday mornings.

The Universe: Accident or Design?

WHAT THE ARGUMENT between believers and unbelievers boils down to is whether the universe is here by accident or by design — whether it has a purpose and an end, or whether it simply happened.

Most scientists, though not all, believe it simply happened. They cannot prove this, any more than religious folk can prove that the Biblical accounts of creation are true, even in the sense of metaphor.

Although my prejudice falls on the side of the believers (but not in a way they would appreciate), I am equally convinced that if hard evidence of a purposeful Creator is ever found, it will be found by science and not by any other means.

Consider, for example, the cosmic-radiation background reports emanating from the Bell Telephone laboratories. Radiation is a "relic" of the state of the universe one second after its expansion got under way. The temperature of that radiation controlled the rate of interaction between protons and neutrons, in much the same way that the heat of a fire controls the way in which it burns.

As Sir Bernard Lovell, the eminent radio astronomer, has said: "It is an astonishing reflection that if the interaction were only a few percent stronger, then all the hydrogen in the primeval condensate would have turned into helium in the stages of expansion. In that case," he continues, "no galaxies, no stars, no life, would have emerged; it would be a universe forever unknowable to living creatures."

There are diverse other such "coincidences" that depend upon a million-to-one chance — such as the curious molecular composition of water, without which no sort of life could be sustained. Just the tiniest change in the disposition of molecules would have doomed the earth to total deadness, if ice sank instead of floating as it does.

Of course, I recognize that the so-called argument from design is not a valid proof of purpose in creation, for if none of these strange coincidences had taken place, we would not be here to know about them. Nonetheless, I find the cunning intricacies of Nature to be powerfully persuasive, if not logically airtight.

The more we learn about the cosmos, the more illuminating and the more mysterious it becomes at the same time. The besetting sin of religion has been its historical resistance to scientific investigation; and the scientific community has returned the insult by slighting or ignoring immaterialist theories. It is hard not to agree with Einstein's balanced judgment: "Science without religion is lame; religion without science is blind."

Human History Has Just Begun

SOME PEOPLE, known as the apocalyptics, see the end of the world approaching within years or decades, in line with their interpretation of Biblical prophesy. I see human history as only just beginning.

The apocalyptics are convinced that time is closing down on us, and that the human race will soon be facing its ultimate destiny on earth. The invention of the nuclear bomb seems to lend some credence to their view.

My own view is through the other end of the binoculars. Human history, as such, is only a few thousand years old. The most ancient calendars we keep — Chinese or Hebrew — are no more than a minute in time, compared to the geological age of the earth, not to mention the astronomical age of the universe.

An intelligent species — if you grant that we are — has inhabited this planet for only a small fraction of its existence. For millions of years before that, the Maker was busy manufacturing manifold other forms of life.

And beyond us, there are billions of other stars and planets in galaxies too distant to glimpse even with the most powerful telescopes at our command.

To insist that we alone are the absolute center, and the ultimate end, of the Creator's cosmic handiwork, strikes me as the most arrogant and anthropocentric delusion we could have. It does not magnify or glorify the concept of creation, but shrinks it to a nearly inconspicuous speck of dirt revolving in an obscure solar system tucked away in a tiny corner of the universe.

My deity is far grander than this, with an infinitely greater reach of time and space. As the most recent of creatures we can know about, a genuine religious humility would compel us to remain silent about the final purpose of the cosmos until we understand more about its workings.

I can conceive of other humans to be created ten thousand or more years from now, who are much closer to the image that God is laboring to bring forth: a species of people who correspond more closely to the visions held by the ancient prophets of nearly all religions.

Time, in our perspective, is not coming to an end; it is only beginning. We are but the rough draft of what humans are meant to be; and if this experiment does not succeed, I do not doubt that the Creator will keep trying until He shapes a model nearer to His heart and mind. It is the apocalyptics who lack faith in His ingenuity, and His scope.

It is almost impossible for modern societies to believe that the concept of romantic love — so pervasive at every level in our lives — was an invention of the Middle Ages, and scarcely recognized as a basic emotion for the first thousand years of recorded civilization.

■

Lay people fail to grasp what a theory is in scientific terms; to dismiss something as "only a theory," as opposed to an "established fact," is to misconstrue the nature of the scientific enterprise.

■

Mere diligence can never do in a dozen years what talent does in a day; yet, at the same time, talent without diligence keeps squandering its inheritance and soon goes bankrupt.

Everything Is Relative . . . to What?

IF YOU HEAR SOMEONE make the remark, "Everything is relative," don't even bother to disagree. Just walk away, and save your breath to cool your porridge, as my mother used to say. Because if you bothered to ask him, "Relative to what?" he could only answer, "Relative to one another," which makes no sense at all and is simply a way to avoid making judgments.

If pressed, such persons may wave vaguely in the direction of Einstein's "theory of relativity" as a prime example, but they don't know what they are talking about.

In his *Scientific Autobiography,* the great German physicist Max Planck wrote that "The often-heard phrase 'Everything is relative' is both misleading and thoughtless. Everything that is relative presupposes the existence of something absolute. Einstein's theory of relativity, too, is based on something absolute — which is the speed of light."

The only way to judge the relation of one thing to another is by using a third thing, which is not relative. The terms *hotter* and *colder* are meaningless without a standard of *absolute cold* to measure them by

Terms like *richer* and *poorer* have validity only because we understand what absolute destitution is, and we judge from there up. They are "relative" terms only in the sense that a person may be seen to be rich in one culture or society, and poor in another, because all societies are relative in wealth. But absolute deprivation is where we start from.

Women are "prettier" or "homelier" only because each of us has a private image of what ultimate beauty should be, even though this is subjective and we may not agree on the standards. Yet without this absolute image, we should be unable to judge any beauty contest.

Much harm has been done to popular thinking by Einstein's

use of the phrase *theory of relativity.* He meant that all events are relative to the individual's time and place, but every event in the universe has reference to the speed of light, which is the same everywhere.

All measurements or comparisons between things must have a third term — expressed or implied — to which they are juxtaposed. Indeed, the supreme goal of the whole scientific inquiry, as Planck says, "is to discover the absolute which alone makes meaningful whatever is given as relative."

Always Remember You Might Be Wrong

HERE WE ARE, two thousand years and more since the Hebrew prophets and the Greek philosophers and the Roman moralists, and we still don't know the best way to rear a child into adulthood. We are still writing books and devising programs and advancing theories and disputing about the attitudes and treatments that are most likely to turn out the kind of sons and daughters who will be a comfort to their families and an adornment to their societies.

With all the experience of the past behind us, with all the multifarious examples and experiments to draw upon, with all our personal knowledge and professional judgment, still no one can say with assurance that there is any single rule or regimen that will apply even to children within the same family.

This being the case, it puzzles me that anyone can be dogmatic about the larger issues of the social order — about politics or economics or international relations. How can we take firm positions on the best arrangements or the smoothest relationships in these vast arenas, when we cannot even predict with any degree of accuracy how any of our children will respond to a particular form or mode of governance?

Of course, we must take positions, but not inflexible ones. Our codes may be absolute, but their application should always be relative to the specific situation. Each system, like each child, has its own strengths and its own deficits. This is why our durable Constitution has been amended twenty-three times and will continue to be so; even the sacred Talmud makes provision for change when ethically necessary.

(What we call capitalism, for instance, is hardly recognizable now as the same creature Adam Smith wrote about; what we call communism today is a tragic parody of what Marx envisioned, no less than what Lenin and Trotsky hoped it might evolve into.)

One hears ideologues of all shades throwing words at one another, as if the words were the objects themselves — even when the objects are no longer what the disputants imagine them to be. Consider for a moment how the concept of discipline has changed over the centuries, from the original disciples of Jesus to the modern advocacy of spanking children.

In his plea to the General Assembly of the Church of Scotland, Oliver Cromwell said, "I beseech you, in the bowels of Christ, think it possible you may be mistaken." When will we learn that the greatest errors in history are made by those who refuse to believe they may be mistaken?

A child is not spoiled by giving him what he wants nearly so much as by giving him substitutes for what he really wants — attention, interest, and understanding.

■

Despite nearly a half-century of research and the millions of dollars poured into it, the field of educational psychology has yet to come up with one workable solution to the problems of mass education in a democratic society.

Can We Combine Realism and Idealism?

ONE OF THE MOST common antitheses that we are fond of making is between the person we call the realist and the one we call the idealist. We customarily look upon these two types as opposites, and in most cases they are.

Yet the older I get, the more convinced I become that our species will not reach its final level of development until and unless these two types become integrated into one. Each alone is as ineffectual as the single blade of a scissors for cutting a straight line.

The realist who subordinates ideals to the practical purposes of a project is more likely in the end to pervert his aims than to fulfill them. Not only does the end not justify any means, but the means we use can corrupt the ends so that they are never realized — Soviet Communism stands as a prime example of so-called realism that has totally crushed idealism.

On the other hand, the pure idealist is equally incapable of reaching his goal, if his estimation of human nature is as absurdly high as the realist's is cynically low. If he asks of people more than they are able to give, he will invariably be disappointed in their failure to meet his standards. (This, by the way, is why so many youthful idealists shrivel into cynics in later life.)

What is required of us, and what is so rare, is a delicate equilibrium between these two polarities, which does not regard people as either angels or brutes, but recognizes our dual nature and is willing to work within the limits of that nature. Lincoln perhaps stands as the paradigm of the public man who was both a consummate politician and an unswerving standard-bearer of man's widest hopes and dreams.

Realism, as it is called, too often degenerates into mere opportunism, while idealism just as often collapses into futility by its failure to accept and deal with our corruptibility. What is needed is to maintain a constant tension between these concepts, not letting go of either end at any time.

The human race has not yet learned the art of combining opposites into a working synthesis; we tend to push each single doctrine to its extreme: The realist becomes an advocate of *Machtpolitik,* and the idealist turns into a crank who cannot tolerate the infirmities of mankind. Each accuses the other of social myopia, and neither can see the distortion in his own viewpoint.

And so the world perpetually oscillates between the damage done to reality by the visionary and the disillusionment done to ideals by the practical men of affairs, each holding a hemisphere and calling it a globe.

Helping Yourself in Order to Help Others

ONE OF THE MOST dangerous and double-edged proverbs in every language is "God helps those who help themselves." As a French wit once added, "but God help those who are *caught* helping themselves."

The trap lies in the ambiguity of the phrase *help themselves.* This has two meanings, each directly opposite to the other: One is the meaning of Christmas; the other is the meaning of our ordinary everyday selfishness.

In one sense of the saying, we are obligated to help ourselves by our own exertions and efforts, by doing all we can to make the most of ourselves and not living off someone else's toil. No one except the truly incapacitated deserves a free ride through life.

In a deeper sense, however, when this basic obligation is met, we help ourselves the most by helping others reach this same level of self-sufficiency and self-respect. In this way, and this way only, we expand our personal egos instead of shrinking, and extend the brief mortality of our lives.

Obviously, if you are not willing to help yourself, you are not then capable of helping others; but self-help is a *means,* and not an *end;* and when it turns into an end (as it does with most of us), its greatest good is transformed into the basest evil.

When we complain that Christmas has become a commercial holiday, we are recognizing the struggle between the forces of good and evil, between the giving that is merely a display of material self-indulgence and pride and vanity, and the giving that is prompted by self-denial and identification with the whole suffering family of mankind.

This is what Christmas is all about; this is what Christianity is all about; indeed, this is what any genuine religion is all about. The root *religio* means "to bind," and the bond is not merely between man and God but between all persons, no matter what they may believe or think they believe — or fail to believe.

Any religion smaller than this is idolatry; and idolatry, of course, is what most of us practice at Christmas, paying homage to the false gods of self-aggrandizement and self-satisfaction — and implicitly teaching our children to be greedy more than grateful.

God may help those who help themselves, but not if they help themselves to more than they are entitled to, or if this is their ultimate goal. Christmas, to mean anything, should be more than an exchange of gifts with those we care for — it must be a response to the needs of those whom the Son of Man lived and died for.

We can save people from external evils, but nobody can be saved from himself if he wants to ruin his life with drink or dope — and all such futile efforts merely add to the numbers of bureaucratic jobholders and subtract huge sums from the public treasury.

Why I Don't Write About Politics

EVERY YEAR, the letters pile up from readers who want to know why I don't write more about political problems and issues, as most other commentators do. When I answer them, I always ask how much they have ever been influenced by a commentator who expresses views very different from theirs. What they are looking for — what most people are looking for — is a *confirmation* of their prior beliefs, not a questioning or rejection of them.

Swift once observed, "You cannot reason a person out of something he has not been reasoned into" — and, of course, most of us have not been reasoned into our basic political and social and economic attitudes. We have adopted them often unconsciously, as a result of our early conditioning and experience; they come from habit, custom, background, prejudice, financial status, and ethnic origin, among other things.

We believe what we find comforting and convenient to believe and then seek rational justification of our opinions. This is why most political dialogue is so full of abstractions about "freedom" and "justice" and "equality" and "opportunity" and all such catchwords.

We inherit or assimilate our opinions in these matters, and then we turn them into frozen systems and ironclad theories; and it makes little difference whether they are royalist or Marxist, for every system is finally shipwrecked on the contradictions and conflicts within the human personality.

My concern is with the basic values necessary to sustain society, and with the underlying attitudes of individuals, not with the glorious abstractions they may publicly proclaim.

I am convinced that political problems can never be resolved on the political level — or by political leaders — but only when enough people in any social order understand its own motives and recognize its own truest needs.

It is only when we cut below the level of politics, and seek a common set of values on which to base our actions, that we have any chance of surviving and flourishing as a permanent species on this globe. Politics divides us; if it rests on little more than prejudice, passion, and partisanship, it can now extinguish us, parties, systems, theories, nations, and all.

Man must get to know himself better, both to appreciate his potentialities and to accept his limitations. He must be offered the chance, somehow, to escape from his bondage to the dreadful abstractions by which he lives, and for which he often dies. *Outlook* must be shaped and guided by *insight*.

Nothing else, at bottom, is worth writing about. And nothing else is truly serious, no matter how solemn or portentous it may appear in print.

My aversion to most vegetables is based on the conviction that while I am bound to serve my country, I am not obliged to eat it.

■

The "loner" may be respected, but he is always resented by his colleagues, for he seems to be passing a critical judgment on them, when he may be simply making a limiting statement about himself.

■

Just about the only interruption we don't object to is applause.

■

Nostalgia for what we once knew is never as acute or persistent as nostalgia for what we feel we missed while it was going on.

■

When Fortune seems to smile, make sure she is not smirking.

Young people exchange greetings; middle-aged people exchange civilities; old people exchange infirmities.

■

Millions of people are willing to die for a faith who have no idea of how to live up to it.

■

How does it happen that so many men who preach the creed of "individualism" are scarcely distinguishable from one another, in appearance, interests, or opinions?

■

"Truth" is usually symbolized as a beacon, but it is really more like a fog-light, which pierces through the fog but does not disperse it.

■

When a parishioner is pleased with a sermon, he has been listening to the wrong sermon; for if one leaves church feeling self-satisfied, the time could just as profitably have been spent on the golf course.

■

The truth is retained in the mind by dramatizing it in our memory; but when we dramatize it, we distort it — and then it is no longer the same truth we vowed to remember.

■

One of the greatest myths is that sports "promotes" international amity, when in fact it does exactly the opposite, and every year it becomes more the agency of national pride and less the symbol of individual merit.

PART III

OF THE
MIND AND PASSIONS

The Joy of Daughters

IT IS NOT HARD to understand why, in primitive or poor societies, the parents generally preferred to have more boy-children than girl-children, for sheer muscle power provided an economic advantage in the struggle for survival.

What is harder to understand is why this preference persists in modern society, even in such an advanced country as the United States, where these economic considerations are negligible. For some, there seems to be more pride and sense of fulfillment when a male is produced — and even the mother herself may share in this satisfaction.

Yet actually, in social and emotional terms, it is the girls who "make" the family more than the boys do, and who supply both the spark and the current in the domestic circuitry. This thought was vividly brought home to me again last Christmas.

With only the two boys home, Christmas might as well have been Groundhog Day, for all the spirit and activity it evoked. As soon as the two girls arrived, however, the whole household came alive, in the fullest sense of the word — with bright sights and laughing sounds and good smells and the bustle of shopping and planning and party-giving and party-going.

As the dreadful poetaster put it, "It takes a heap o'living to make a house a home," but he should have added that most of that living is generated and sustained by the distaff side of the family. Nor is it merely that the females do the cooking and the decorating; it is, rather, that they act as the "binder" in the family, like the eggs in batter or the gum in paint.

Boys are splendid creatures, and I would not want to be without a son, but there is nothing like a daughter when a man feels low or tired and a young nymph comes up behind his chair and kisses him on the back of the head for no other reason than she feels like it. That's when every day is Christmas.

In my fathering years, whenever someone would ask me the foolish question, "Do you want a boy or a girl?" I would always answer "Yes" — for what I wanted was a boy or a girl, and not a bird or a baboon. It mattered not a bit to me, but now, in my early senescence, I would feel keenly deprived had I not been blessed with a daughter.

It may not be a manifestation of male chauvinism that so many husbands covet a son and heir, but it is certainly a form of male stupidity. A son may bring honor and pride to his family, but for comfort and consolation and cheerfulness in the house, there is nothing that can beat a daughter.

Why Parents Live for Their Children

WHEN MY ELDER SON was about fifteen, he once said to me, "There's something I don't understand, Dad. If parents live for their children, and their children live for *their* children, and so on — when do you ever start living for yourself?"

This seemed to him an endless process, with no final goal in view. Although I knew it might be hard for him to grasp at that age, I sat down and tried to explain how and why most parents feel this way about their children, and why it is not looked upon as an endless treadmill.

People cultivate crops and flowers. They plant trees whose

fullness they will never live to see. They compose music and paint pictures and write books — and a large part of the gratification is the hope that these creations will outlive them and give some pleasure or profit to future generations.

Since most individuals lack the special talent to fabricate works of art or any reminders testifying to their existence, children have remained the prime way of expressing this deep human need for continuity with the future. Parenthood, among other things, represents our wish to remain connected with the process of human history.

Now, just as a writer or composer or painter wants to produce a work that epitomizes the best of himself, free from most of the dross of his actual life, so does a parent want to rear children who are better than he is — who are more of what human beings could be and ought to be: freer to love and more worthy of being loved.

We aim at idealized versions of ourselves, lacking the defects and blemishes and scars we have carried through much of our lifetimes. We would like them to enjoy more and suffer less, to realize themselves more fully in more dimensions than we have been able to.

Most couples yearn for children not merely to gratify their vanity but also because of the conscious or unconscious recognition that a person who lives only for his own time has little meaning in the total scheme of things; most of us obtain a kind of immortality only by producing and cultivating something that promises to outlive our brief span on earth.

Parenthood is our paramount way of confronting, and partly subduing, "that bloody tyrant Time" and binding past and present to the future. In one sense, it is a ceaseless movement from generation to generation, sometimes ebbing and sometimes cresting; but because it has no ending does not mean it has no point. The point is in the process itself, just as the "end" of life is the living of it.

Keeping Friendships in Repair

ONE THING WE LEARN, or should learn, as we grow older is to keep our friendships in repair; otherwise they deteriorate with time and weather, just like a neglected fence.

One of my biggest regrets is a friendship I failed to keep in repair, some years ago, for the usual insufficient reasons — lack of time, too many other concerns, travel, and family affairs. Then, when I finally got around to it, my friend had died while I was out of town and I learned about it only later. This was a bitter experience, because he needed old friends in his last, struggling year, and I was not there to give even moral support. This remains an indelibly black mark against my character.

Friends of long standing become even more necessary as we start the long slope downward, and other elements in our life begin to recede. Children marry and move away; jobs diminish in activity and importance; ill health may become pervasive, and we feel the world slowly slipping through our fingers. In the end, sharing common memories is much of what is left. "Oldtimers" tend to reminisce so much because it connects the past with the present and provides a sense of continuity through time, with some permanence of identity. It is the only way of "belonging" that remains.

What many fail to recognize is that friendship lies more in quality than in quantity. I have attended the funerals of some famous persons, where thousands were in attendance — and yet I knew that these celebrities were basically alone in their personal lives; their multitude of "friends" consisted largely of hangers-on, merrymakers, adulators, little fish who wanted to be in the swim and would quickly seek another whale to follow to another cove.

If we have three or four friends, whose ties go back through days of adversity, we are more fortunate than most. And if we fail to make new friends of this enduring stripe as we go through life, we will find that death or distance has sadly diminished their numbers.

No one really understands friendship, any more than we understand a romantic affinity. It is more, and different, than a meeting of minds, a conjunction of interests, a similarity of backgrounds, though it may include all these things.

One of my dearest friends disagreed with me about almost everything in the world — the only thing we agreed upon was that we liked, enjoyed, and trusted each other. If you have this, you don't need anything else; and if you don't, nothing else matters.

Being Yourself Is Just a Beginning

THE GRATUITOUS ADVICE given to so many people, "Be yourself," is useful only for a start; it is terrible advice if it is mistaken as a goal, as it usually is. Most persons who seek advice would like to develop their personalities, in one way or another. Telling them to "Be yourself" is no help whatsoever, unless it is explicated with more useful counseling.

What this phrase means, or should mean, is "Begin with yourself and work out from there." It means do not try to be somebody else, somebody imitative, somebody inauthentic to your own disposition and background.

Your *self* is where and what you start from, and you build on it, finding your own strengths and shoring up your weaknesses as self-examination makes them evident to you. Being yourself, however, does not mean accepting only what you are at this particular stage of life. It means using it as a jumping-off place.

Growth and development are the aim of every organism, and while what we call the "self" has a core that cannot be denied or repudiated without grave danger to the whole organism, a personality acquires different layers and levels of adjusting to life, different modes of coping with difficulties.

All these layers and levels and modes, however, must arise out of the authentic core of the person, or they are eventually perceived as mere postures and devices to protect our felt vulnerability.

The persons we most admire and are willing to trust are those who seem most natural to us — which indicates that they have built their responses on the core that is within them, and not on some model they have borrowed from fiction or a fantasy fabricated in their own quest for wish-fulfillment.

Every person who is born has his or her own integrity and identity and as much inner worth as any other. Our job is much like mining: to dig into ourselves and bring this inner worth to the surface. In so doing, we will bring up a lot of detritus also, and the rest of our job is learning what to keep and what to discard.

Being yourself is not remaining what you were, or being satisfied with what you are. It is the point of departure and far from the goal. It is working with what you have and what has helped shape you in your heredity and environment; it is the root, not the branches, much less the flower.

Nobody is enough, in a human sense, or all he could be. Socrates learned to dance when he was seventy, because he felt that essential part of himself had been neglected. We are born, of course, with different limitations; but scarcely anyone lives up to those limitations. The least we can do is try to die up to them. Then you know you have really been yourself.

Two Lives Wouldn't Be Enough

MANY PEOPLE ARE FOND OF REFLECTING that they would like a chance to live their lives over again, so that they could avoid the mistakes they made the first time. I have never been able to believe this would do much good.

In my opinion, most of us would need at least three lives, not two, in order to profit from our flaws and follies: the first in which to commit our initial errors, the second in which to commit exactly the opposite ones, and the third in which to strike a reasonable balance between these extremes.

Most of us, given the time and opportunity, learn from our mistakes only to go in the opposite direction: The person who is bruised by his naïveté turns cynical the next time; the trusting person, once betrayed, turns unduly suspicious; the repressed person, once released, wallows in sensuality.

Poor people who suddenly strike it rich generally have no notion of how to handle their new wealth and turn as profligate as they were formerly prudential. Egalitarians, when they assume the reins of authority, become more dictatorial than those they have ousted. (The French Revolution is only the most dramatic example in history.)

And, of course, the religious zealot who calls for "liberty of conscience" when he is persecuted has a notorious record of persecuting others when given the power and opportunity.

A second chance at life would not suffice for most of mankind. When we learn that something is wrong, we tend to assume that its opposite is right. We view circumstances in terms of contradictions instead of complementaries; we separate into rigid compartments those attitudes and approaches that must be blended and joined to obtain our optimum satisfaction.

In social theory, for example, if "coddling" our convicts doesn't work, then we adopt harsh measures, ignoring the plain fact that neither kindness nor cruelty alone is an effectual treatment and that rehabilitation must be based on some understanding of their inner dynamics and social conditioning.

If world peace has thus far failed because we have not worked out a proper system of conflict resolution, we arm ourselves to the teeth, making another global war nearly inevitable, because we have found no path between mutual defense and naked aggression. This, of course, is the ultimate folly of mankind.

No, I am afraid that two lives would not be sufficient to turn us into rational creatures. Three might just possibly do it, and then again might not. We are the victims of our emotions, endowed with the kind of intellect that persuades us to justify our appetites by selecting only those "reasons" that serve our gratification. It is not our animal passions that betray us as much as our minds themselves, which cater to our impulses while pretending to control them.

What Makes a Successful Marriage?

WE CAN PREDICT, with some confidence, that certain marriages are almost doomed to fail. We can predict, though not quite so confidently, that some others have good prospects for success. What we cannot prophesy is the great bulk of marriages, where neither failure nor success seems preordained.

Marriage is an equation with too many variables to tote up accurately — age, background, temperament, social status, mental levels, family pressures, career choices, sexual drives, attitudes toward children, and even political and religious convictions.

All these factors interlock, either meshing or grinding, and no one can know how much weight to give to each in relation to the others or how each party will react to the balance between pleasure and pressure — not even the marital partners themselves, and perhaps they least of all.

One of the newest professions in the country is that of family counseling, which I would not undertake for all the uranium in Canada. For it is an indisputable fact that some of the most improbable unions last for a lifetime, and some "made in Heaven" are rapidly unmade in Hell. If all the advice given young people about to marry were laid end to end, everyone might be better off. At best, such advice has more negative than positive value.

We in the West laugh or sneer at or reproach the old custom in India of parents' arranging a marriage between teenagers who may not yet have even met one another. But there is no hard evidence that such arranged marriages are, on the whole, less successful or happy or enduring than our own.

One reason for this, perhaps, is that "happiness" as such is not one of the main criteria for a good marriage in the East. Nor was it in the West until this century. If someone had asked my mother if she was "happy" in her marriage, she would have thought the questioner crazy. As it so happened, she was, but the thought would not have occurred to her. You didn't marry to be happy; that was a by-product; if it came, it was something extra; if not, you shrugged and made do.

I am far from defending the indissolubility of marriage, especially where there are "irreconcilable differences" between the mates. I am simply suggesting that every choice is more or less a blind one (or sometimes an actually perverse one), and that the selection by parents is not as absurd or despotic as it may seem in our eyes.

In this land and era of "rising expectations," our expectations for marriage have risen along with our social and economic ambitions. But greater freedom to choose has not necessarily been accompanied by better judgment in choosing, and all we can rightly say is that we prefer making our own mistakes to having them made for us by others.

Nine tenths of the troubles in marital or parental relationships come from a refusal to let the other person be who he or she is, in trying to turn a reality into a fantasy, instead of abandoning the fantasy for the reality.

Kicking a Man When He's Down

THERE IS AN OLD SAYING, "You don't kick a man when he's down," but that is more a pious hypocrisy than a rule of action for most people. When someone is down is often the most irresistible time for kicking.

"Down" can mean a lot of different things. It can mean someone who is weak and vulnerable, or someone who does not fit in, or someone who seems conspicuously a failure, in terms of money, status, or even personal attractiveness.

We are impressed with those who radiate strength, security, and self-confidence, and seek to draw a certain kind of magnetism from them — just as we tend to avoid persons who exude the aroma of failure, which we suppose is "catching," in the same way a disease may be contagious.

Some atavistic element in our nature shuns, ridicules, and rejects whatever is different or deviant from our own standards or ideals, whether that deviation is in culture or class or language or color or even some individual quirk of character. In that sense, we are all xenophobic.

We can see it most easily in children, who goad and tease any classmate bearing some infirmity, or whatever is considered a blemish or defect that sets him or her apart from the others.

What we are reluctant to recognize, however, is that when we sneer or mock or reject, we are diminishing ourselves in the act of demeaning another for a flaw he cannot help or was born with or acquired through a deprived or perverted upbringing.

Deficiencies in others seem to bring out the worst in us, rather than the best; and most differences are perceived as deficiencies. Looking down makes us feel larger and stronger. We are compassionate only when we feel we can afford it — and then only toward those who do not seem to threaten our social values or damage our self-esteem.

This is largely why we send millions to starving Ethiopian babies, while we ignore deprivation on our own doorstep. Of course, the Ethiopians need it more, but it is also easier to provide "charity" to strangers thousands of miles away than to treat our own unfortunates humanely.

We are willing to reproach ourselves for being egocentric, but ethnocentricity is just as sinful, and philanthropy abroad is no substitute for neighborliness at home; and we are neighborly only toward those who share our background and conform to our notion of acceptability.

An unfortunate across the ocean is a "victim"; an unfortunate across town is a "failure." By persisting in this posture, we in the mainstream run the risk of being the greatest failures of all.

When the Truth Hurts

WHAT DOES IT MEAN to "know" something? On the surface, this seems to be an obvious and even stupid question. Surely we know when we know something, as opposed to when we only surmise or suspect it. Or do we?

When a former Nazi concentration camp guard is brought to trial here to face deportation charges, for instance, it is common for him to say he "didn't know" what was taking place in the camp. He lived nearby, and only stamped papers or signed vouchers, and had nothing to do with the gas ovens.

Such persons have been studied by Yale psychiatrist Robert Jay Lifton, who came to the conclusion that there is such a thing as "middle knowledge," a form of self-delusion that all of us indulge in when circumstances seem to make it necessary. This middle knowledge is a distortion of memory to fit what we would like to believe or have been conditioned to believe.

Lifton cited one doctor, among others, who was involved in shipping large amounts of cyanide to the Nazi death camps and was quite genuinely shocked when told the poison had been used to exterminate people. As Lifton tersely put it: "He worked very hard not to know." Likewise, most of the Germans who lived near these camps made themselves "unaware" of what was going on only a dozen miles away.

These people are not lying or fabricating, in any conscious sense of the word. In a recent book on "Memory," the author reported an experiment in which the subjects were shown a picture of several passengers on a subway train, which included a black man wearing a hat, and a white man with an open razor in his hand.

The experimenters then asked the first subject to transmit this information to the next person, and so on down the line — like the children's game of "telephone" — and by the time the picture was received by the later subjects, the razor had migrated in memory from the white man to the black man.

In this case, stereotypes of racial behavior are influencing what people "see" and what they "remember." Knowing and remembering are not so much acts of the eye or of the memory as reconstructions of the mind, based on our assumptions, our prejudices, our social conditioning, and our need to feel comfortable with ourselves.

These distortions are what psychologists call constructive errors and are one reason that witnesses so often make mistakes in identifying the culprit in a police line-up. As C. S. Morgan has picturesquely expressed it, "We fill up the lowlands of our memories from the highlands of our imaginations."

Guilty or innocent, those Nazi guards and doctors are not lying — or, if they are, they are lying only to themselves, as we all do when the truth would hurt.

Answers Are Hard to Find

WHY IS THE DEMAND so great for, and the supply so short in, constructive criticism? Whenever two parties are disagreeing, one side invariably calls for the other to engage in constructive criticism.

The fact is that nothing is harder in life than knowing what should be done, for there are dozens of ways to do something wrong, and usually only one way to do it right.

"It is easier to be critical than to be correct," said Disraeli, in rebuking his parliamentary opponents — neglecting to add that this was as true for his own party.

The process of learning consists in collecting "non-answers" rather than in finding answers. We find out the things that don't work through trial and error, usually repeated many times in different ways, before we hit upon the answer, if we ever do.

One of the most common errors is to suppose that the opposite of being wrong is right, when in many cases it is only another way of being wrong. We see this most obviously in political and governmental doctrines, where one extreme proves as futile as the other.

This is why almost every criticism leveled at a regime is more or less valid — but what is proposed in its place is usually just as ineffective.

As an example on the personal level, someone who makes the wrong choice in a marriage will often, after a divorce, choose exactly the opposite kind of person — and then find that this, too, was an egregious mistake.

What we do is collect non-answers as we go through life, learning the things that don't work and hoping we will strike some kind of balance that gives us a reasonable shot at success. The odds are not tilted in our favor, however, and we need as much luck as brains.

The U.S. Constitution required ten amendments before it passed muster, and it is continually being amended to rectify its flaws and omissions and to meet the criticism of the new generations. And there will be no end to these revisions.

In point of fact, "destructive" criticism is as essential as constructive, for it is often necessary to demolish before something can be built in its place. Revolutions always know what they are *against* much more clearly than they know what they are *for* — which is why they so often go wrong and betray the hopes of their founders.

In any debate, the negative always has the better of it, because all human schemes are fallible, and every solution poses other problems that simply have a different set of holes.

Practice May Ingrain Bad Habits

You probably know the chestnut about the stranger in New York, carrying a violin case, who stops an old lady on the street, and asks, "Can you tell me how to get to Carnegie Hall?" With a glance at his violin case, she replies, "Practice, practice, practice!"

One of the oldest maxims in the world is that "Practice makes perfect." This, however, is a dangerous half-truth that has betrayed many novices in many fields of accomplishment.

If you start to learn something the wrong way (which is usually the easiest way), the longer you practice, the more ingrained become your bad habits, and the longer it takes to correct them and get on the proper path.

As an example, a tennis instructor would much rather teach a rank beginner than someone who has been playing casually for years — because the latter has already acquired awkward strokes and faulty footwork, and first has to be made to "unlearn" these responses before he can be taught good form.

(This, by the way, is one reason that adult education is so much harder than child education: We can take the child from ignorance to knowledge, but we must take the adult from error to ignorance before he is ready to accept knowledge.)

Habit is a two-faced value, both a virtue and a vice. Habit allows the typist to let her fingers fly over the keyboard without even thinking about the position of the letters, and this increases her efficiency. At the same time, it has prevented the introduction of a more sensible arrangement of the keyboard — which would save much more time in the long run — because no one wants to sacrifice an acquired skill.

We continue to do things the old way largely because it is more comfortable, and then we make up reasons to justify our unwillingness to change. This is true in almost every area — it is well known to military historians that generals are always fighting the last war, not the current one.

The learning process is dynamic, not static, but most teaching methods tend to look backward, not forward. Practice always lags behind theory, sometimes by as much as a generation, since it is easier for everyone to keep on doing what he has always done than adapt to a new set of circumstances.

The violinist who has been poorly prepared gets not to Carnegie Hall but only into a deeper rut with "practice, practice, practice." Repeating is not learning; it is merely memorizing habits that may threaten to make us their slaves rather than their masters.

The principal difference between a college and a university was defined by Robert Hutchins, when he said: "A college teaches; a university both teaches and learns."

■

People who engage in absurd or backbreaking efforts simply to get their names into the Guinness Book of World Records *fail to understand the Harris Law of Nugatory Achievement, namely: "If a thing isn't worth doing, it isn't worth doing well."*

Not All Knowledge Is Power

"BRAINS IS CHEAP," a self-made tycoon once said to a friend of mine. "I can buy them by the dozen any day."

Ever since Francis Bacon proclaimed that "knowledge is power," we have supposed that learning and education provided the royal road to influence and status. But the knowledge that confers power is quite a different thing.

In every form of society — be it monarchial or republican, capitalistic or socialistic — it is knowledge of *people* that confers power, not knowledge of facts or things. It is knowing how to *manipulate*, not how to theorize or philosophize or compute or analyze.

Power is always able to buy brains, to use them and to discard them when no longer needed. Politically, we can see this with a shrewdly ignorant peasant like Stalin, or a psychopath like Hitler, who commanded some of the finest minds of their countries and their times.

Financially, the men who do best are not necessarily the brainiest, or the best informed, but the canniest in playing on people's appetites and emotions, in pulling strings and pressing nerves and jockeying for position in the competitive arena.

Publicly, we pay lip service to something called education, but privately we accept the fact that most affluent and successful men are indifferent to, or actually contemptuous of, the educated person. Brains are a commodity on the market, to be bought or rented, by those who can afford to — and the price is not always high.

What is required for dominance in the marketplace is a kind of "savvy" — and this savvy has little to do with knowledge in any formal, structured sense of the word.

The men who run Du Pont or AT&T are not scientists or chemists or technicians who necessarily know anything about the abstruse operations of their firms: The men in power hire these brains by the thousands, pay them well when times are good, and lay them off when they feel like it.

It is not just our system; all systems run that way and always have; Shakespeare was wiser than his contemporary Francis Bacon: In one of his earlier sonnets, he refers to the scholar kowtowing to the "gilded fool."

Such men, however, are by no means fools. Quite the contrary: They understand people's motives, their needs and fears and hopes, far better than does the technician or the cloistered academician. This narrow, focused kind of knowledge is what engenders power, from the throne room to the countinghouse.

Words Shape Our Thoughts

THE WORD that has been most cheapened and devalued in our language is *love*. We use it for everything — we "love" our mothers, we "love" our new car, we "love" ice cream and Mozart and picnics and being left alone.

Most people suppose that first we think, and then we find words to express our thoughts. Actually, we think *in* and *with* words, and the words we have at our command shape our thoughts, rather than the other way around.

Although the ancients had fewer words (because there were fewer things in the world), they discriminated more than we do among the ones they had. They had at least three different words to express what we call "love" — there was *philia*, for love of family and friends and countrymen; there was *eros*, for love between the sexes; and there was *agape*, for love of God. They did not apply the word *love* to objects such as chariots and clothing and food and drink and worldly pleasures, for love is not a univocal word. A univocal word is one that has only a single specific meaning and cannot be attached loosely to a wide variety of objects.

Obviously, we do not love our children in the same way we love our wives or sweethearts. We do not love our country in any sense that we love the color blue or the taste of peppermint or the smell of roses. We do not love God in the way we love our pet cockatoo.

Our failure to make these verbal distinctions is more than "a manner of speaking"; it is a manner of conceptualizing, of defining and distinguishing. The words we use control and direct and limit the thoughts they express. We are spurred to action by slogans and catchwords rather than by the concrete realities they embody.

If we "love" the things that give us pleasure, because they give us pleasure, we will stop loving them when they give us pain. But Job's "love" of God had nothing to do with pleasure or pain, happiness or unhappiness; it was wholly on another level of trust and fealty.

Because we use words so loosely and indiscriminately, we are able to justify almost anything we want to do: People who are willful call themselves "independent" and take their defect for a virtue; people who are predatory call their greed "enterprise" and are proud of what they should be ashamed of.

If so distinctive a word as *love* is invariably misused and abused and flattened and coarsened, imagine what we do with language generally, every day in every way. Like Humpty Dumpty, when we use a word, it means just what we choose to make it mean, because the meanings are not in the words themselves, but in the people who use them.

Adults Need Fairy Tales, Too

WATCHING, for a little while, one of the new adventure-and-suspense programs on television, it occurred to me that what the public really wants is a combination of novelty and familiarity, wickedness and morality. In virtually all these shows, the struggle is between good and evil — and good invariably triumphs. We know for a certainty that the hero in a dramatic series will be around next week, and even next year if the series is successful. The suspense is totally fictitious, for the "good guy" is never allowed to die. In the same way, the adventure is basically safe; our deeper layer of consciousness is comfortably aware that, at the end of the episode, the hero will be relatively unscathed and the villain brought to heel. In this basic sense, there is no novelty in the presentation.

Adults are more like children than we care to believe. A child basically seeks reassurance in the stories he is told; in the end, Hansel and Gretel are saved from the witch, and the wolf in grandma's clothes is slain by the woodcutter. (Although in the original folktale, Red Riding Hood was actually devoured.)

In a larger sense, all these cliffhangers, either in books or on the screen, are themselves fairy tales, for we know that in real life, the heroes and the villains are not so clearly defined, and even when they are, the bad guys are as likely to prevail as the good guys.

What we call escape entertainment is escape from a reality we do not care to acknowledge; it is a flight back to childhood, when we know that mother and father are in the next room, no matter how fiercely the wind howls or how menacingly the shadows on the curtains seem to move toward our bed.

Critics are shortsighted in evaluating these dramas as works of art or as paradigms of the human condition. They are, instead, therapeutic devices, designed to provide us with a *frisson* of excitement, while at the same time they guarantee that no real harm will befall us, or people like us. Babies love to scream in fright when Daddy pretends to be a bear, because they know that as he approaches, the bite will turn into a kiss, a hug, or a tickle; and they never tire of this game. It is for the same reason that all adventure stories are really one story, told again and again, to comfort the child in all of us.

Nothing Succeeds Like Success

THERE IS A STORY, well attested to, that Charlie Chaplin once entered a "Charlie Chaplin look-alike" contest — and came in third. Also, that Jascha Heifetz, in the days of his fame, played his violin in the streets, receiving no more attention than any blind fiddler. What is known for a fact, however, is that Enrico Caruso, just for fun, once sang Beppe's offstage serenade in the second act of *Pagliacci,* and received no more applause than would any other — unknown — junior lead. The audience couldn't see, and didn't know, who was singing.

For years, as a young man, I could never understand the meaning of the old saw "Nothing succeeds like success." What it means, of course, is that success carries an impetus of its own, quite apart from the talent involved. If the judges had known it was Chaplin, he would have won the contest. If the passers-by had known it was Heifetz, he would have been mobbed. If the opera audience had known it was Caruso warbling offstage, he would have been deafened with applause.

It is the reputation that is rewarded, more than the exhibition of talent. The name makes the game, in the eyes (and ears) of the public. Fame creates its own generative power of response.

It is not only unknown masterpieces that have been turned down by dozens of book publishers in succession; sometimes, as a bitter joke, an acknowledged masterpiece has been submitted under another name — and has been summarily rejected, without anyone's recognizing the hoax.

A Picasso signed will attract a thousand viewers; an unsigned one by the same artist will be passed by with scarcely a glance, or even sneered at as a poor imitation of the master.

Fritz Kreisler, the violinist, in his early days, played compositions he attributed to old composers who never existed. These were respectfully received, but in later years Kreisler revealed that he himself was the composer, justifying his deception on the ground that the critics would have scoffed at compositions of his own making.

It is the image that we pay homage to, more than the substance. One of Phil Silvers' earliest sketches involved a famous comedian's getting a haircut from a barber who laughs uproariously at every word he utters, even though nothing at all funny has been said.

In Shakespeare, nobody takes the Fool seriously, even when he says the wisest things in the play. But dress him in judicial robes, and when he opens his mouth no dog will dare bark.

Prickly Person Is Soft at Core

SPEAKING OF PEOPLE who are hard to get along with, as I was the other day, it seems to me that hardly anyone really believes this about himself or herself.

If we happen to hear criticism of ourselves, directly or indirectly, we tend to protest that we are misunderstood or that our reactions are misinterpreted by others.

Bobby Burns told us long ago that we cannot see ourselves as others see us, and while we may recognize this as a general axiom, we rarely apply it to ourselves, but only to others. We know that we cannot hear our own voices accurately, or smell our own breaths, but we are reluctant to admit to the same ignorance about the very fabric of personality.

Unfortunately, the world judges us more by surface personality and temperament than by character. A person may have a fine character, but a difficult temperament — yet the temperament is what rubs up against others in the short run, and the virtues of character may not come to light in time to redeem the relationship. In most cases, people are not aware of their abrasiveness, or their rudeness, their curtness, their stubbornness or sarcasm, or whatever temperamental affliction coats the surface of their social lives — and this includes some of the most intelligent and otherwise perceptive people one would care to know. Conversely, of course, there are those with amiable and even alluring temperaments who are woefully deficient in character. They may be easy to get along with because they make as little demand upon themselves as they do upon others. They are liked and approved because they do not ruffle our good opinion of ourselves, even though they may prove to be disappointing in the long run.

Obviously, the ideal is a combination of good character and sweet temperament, but this is as rare as a balanced blend of brains and brawn and beauty. When the different personal assets were dispensed by our Maker, it seems as if care was taken not to grant an abundance of all to any one recipient.

As we grow older we learn compassion toward those with physical failings and do not mock them, as children do. What we need to learn, also, is that temperamental defects can be just as crippling, and to regard their possessors as being as much victims as culprits. Some of the most rewarding persons I have known have been difficult, but, like many obstacles, the obstacle of a prickly personality is often worth overcoming — and, when overcome, in a surprising number of cases, is found to have a gentle core that is protecting itself in the only way it has learned to cope.

Someone who is sick and cheerful arouses our admiration, while someone healthy and depressed merely elicits our annoyance and impatience; but if we could realize that, with the latter, the sadness is their sickness, we might be more sympathetic toward their unattractive ailment.

■

People who are resolutely cheerful can be just as taxing as people who are chronically grumpy.

Children Are Hard to Deceive

IF I SAID TO YOU that most children understand adults better than most adults understand children, your immediate reaction would most likely be incredulity and rejection. After all, children are simple and naïve, and tend to confuse appearance with reality, whereas adult judgments are more subtle and discriminating. But the understanding I refer to is not factual; it is emotional. A child can be deceived by facts; it is much harder to fool a child about feelings. A child is closer to his own feelings than an adult is, and because of this, he or she is able to "pick up," as it were, the true motivations and promptings of adults, beneath the plausible reasons we project to others. That is to say, our unconscious and unexpressed feelings are quite clear to the child (of a certain age, of course), while the child's inner dynamics may be obscure to us, because we have grown so far apart from our own childhood selves and tend to block out our early impressions.

(Every magician on record, for instance, has testified that it is much harder to fool an audience of children than one of adults — for the child keeps his eyes on the object, and cannot easily be misdirected by gesture or patter. In this sense, he is closer to reality than are his parents.)

This attachment to reality has nothing to do with "knowledge" as we define it; it has to do, rather, with being clear-eyed and free from the preconceptions that burden most adults as they grow up and acquire a shell of sophistication. It is precisely because the child remains simple, in an emotional sense, that he or she is able to detect radiations of personality that are beyond the psychic range of the adult.

And this, I think, is what Jesus truly meant when he told us that "Except ye become as little children, ye shall not enter the kingdom of heaven." It was not a religious or an ethical injunction, but a shrewd psychological one: He was saying that we must remain, at the same time, as trusting as children and as keen in detecting the true from the deceptive.

It is easy to deceive a child verbally; it is hard to deceive him visually or emotionally. One reason that children are so close to other animals is that, like animals, they respond to subliminal stimuli; they sense who really likes them and who doesn't; they can distinguish a reason from a rationalization — even when their parents or teachers cannot.

That "a little child shall lead them" is not a sentimental distortion, but a keen perception that in growing up we lose as much as we gain; and the most important thing we lose is our potential for seeing, and even "smelling," the truth about other people. The great tragedy of mankind is that in the process of maturing we relinquish our honesty along with our innocence.

Taking Sides Is a Human Tendency

IT IS INTERESTING to note how people are propelled toward partisanship even when they have no primary interest in the outcome of a contest. My two sons were watching a football game on TV some weeks ago, and obviously rooting for one of the teams. I asked them why, since neither was a local team, and they both shrugged and lamely fabricated some reason or other; finally, one of them said in candor, "Well, you know, Dad, it's just more fun watching when you can take sides."

This is a harmless attitude in sporting contests, but I think it represents a widespread human tendency that gets us into trouble more often than not. There is no psychological challenge or excitement in remaining neutral; lack of partisanship is boring compared to the fervor of cheering for a favorite. Taking sides gives one a feeling of *belonging,* which is evidently one of the most forceful drives of the human animal. It forms the core of everything from a gang and an army to a political party. No matter how much "individualism" we may preach philosophically, in emotional terms we have a deep need to identify ourselves with some specific goal.

And I would suggest that the passion for sporting events — in which everybody is "for" one team or another, no matter how temporary or factitious that team may be — is a substitution for the frustrated sense of loyalty most people feel about the larger issues of life. Disillusionment with politics and government generally, and the pandemic cynicism about most leaders, has left the average person feeling empty and unattached. Since there are fewer and fewer things in public life that one can believe in wholeheartedly, the vacuum must be filled with surrogate loyalties to some sporting aggregation that seems to win on sheer merit, not on cunning and duplicity.

(This is why an athletic scandal — the "fixing" of a baseball game, the "shaving" of football points, or the "tanking" of a boxer — shocks the sporting public all out of proportion to its importance: because it debases the arena to the level of corrupt business or political practices.)

Since so many of the things we are supposed to believe in have proved unworthy of belief, we have retreated into the miniature world of sports and expend our loyalties there — even if we have to manufacture them for the occasion. It is too much to suppose that we will ever find as much pleasure in neutrality as we do in commitment.

May it be said of us what was said of Viscount Asquith upon his death: "If he was sometimes on the wrong side, he was never on the side of wrong."

■

Almost all men who play poker suffer from the delusion that they are better players than they are — and their really good opponents are careful to say nothing to discourage this conceit.

What Age Suits You?

STEPHEN SPENDER, the British poet, was seventy-five years old on February 28, 1984, and upon that occasion he was interviewed by the editor of *The New York Times Book Review*. In reply to the birthday congratulations, Spender said, "The funny thing about old age is the way it suddenly steals up on you. . . . You wake up and you're seventy-five and you wonder how you got there."

The poet then quoted Freud's observation that "subconsciously you remain the same age throughout your life," and added that he still felt to be an adolescent, which is perhaps one reason he got along so well with his undergraduate students.

I remember how dreadfully old my teachers seemed to me when I was still in school, although actually many of them were scarcely middle-aged. Spender felt the same way when he first met T. S. Eliot, although the "older man" was only just forty.

People age at different rates and in different ways. I have long held the theory that each person has his or her "optimum age," just as all of us have our optimum weight. We reach this optimum at different times in our lives, and then stay this way permanently.

In my own case, I was impatient all during my youth to become thirty-five, and when I reached it I stopped aging "inside." My mental image of myself is still thirty-five, and it surprises me when my body rebels at this arrogant assumption. Internally, I feel not a whit older than I did then — except when I am rash enough to climb more than one flight of stairs.

Conversely, I have known people who did not feel comfortable with themselves until they were old, whose whole lives seemed to be waiting for them to achieve the ripeness of age and beyond. They seemed to spend their lives marking time for the years to catch up with them.

Others, more numerous perhaps, were the "Peter Pan" types who never wanted to grow up, and who resented the obligations imposed upon them by adulthood. Their minds and spirits did not seem to grow with them, and their efforts to remain young became more desperate — and more pitiable — with the years.

And some people never seem to find their optimum age, in a psychological sense. As youths, they want to be older; in middle age, they want the prerogatives but not the responsibilities; and in old age, they yearn for what they feel they missed at other stages.

Everyone is enjoined to "act your age" — but what if the age you are at is not the age you feel within yourself? And it rarely is.

Marriage Is a Process

THE MOST COMMON explanation given by couples who separate or divorce is that one or the other, or both, "changed" after the marriage. I suspect that, in most cases, this is exactly the opposite of the real reason. I think it is because one or the other, or both, *refused* to change. If the partners did not change in marriage, then no marriage could persist for very long. If each of the parties remained as he or she was in the beginning, the whole institution would collapse into a heap of rubble.

We speak of the "marital state" — but it is not a state, or a condition; it is a *process*. Most of all, it is a learning process: In it, you gradually learn who the other party is, and at the same time you learn who you are. As in all learning, it is partly a pleasure and partly a pain, and the less the partners are aware of their true identities, the more the pain.

William James said that there are six personalities involved in every such relationship: What he thinks he is, what she thinks he is, and what he really is; and conversely, what she thinks she is, what he thinks she is, and what she really is. All these disparate and delusional personalities need to be sorted out as a marriage progresses, and it takes time and patience above all. The lesson is never completely finished, just as learning anything is never completely finished.

Change may not be the name of the game, but it is the first and almost the last rule of the game. Not a change of character, which is impossible, or even a change in temperament, which is almost as hard, but a change in habits, in attitudes, in reactions and responses.

No one is ready for marriage, just as no one is ready for any new stage in life, be it adolescence or senility. Every stage calls for a drastic adjustment in perspective. Heraclitus said that we never step into the same river twice — and the waters of matrimony require as much balance and dexterity as canoeing down a rapids.

It is not that people change in marriage that causes estrangement; it is that they do not. They retain their old habits, cherish their old prejudices, preserve their old values, and cling to the fanciful notion that love conquers all. But love, as Bruno Bettelheim has warned, is not enough; and love without understanding is a knife turned against itself. What must be understood most of all is that if we are not willing to change, if we see no reason to change, then we stop learning and stop growing — and, eventually, stop loving.

Who changes what, and how much, and in what ways, are matters of individual perceptions and judgments and nice accommodations. Love is necessary in marriage not as a romantic overlay, but because even with it, marriage is hard and perilous. Without it, there is no way to shoot those rapids.

Do What You Do Best

THE ONLY ADVICE I ever give to young people who come to me for career counseling consists of ten one-syllable words: "Find out what you do best, and stick with it."

No failure in life is as final or implacable as the failure to find out what you do best. For there is at least one worthy thing that we can do better than most people — and whatever this aptitude or ability may be, it is the thing we should be doing.

Also, in a certain sense, this activity must come naturally and easily. This does not mean that hard work and long practice may be avoided, but it does mean that the work will be as much a pleasure as a chore, and that practice will seem more than simply drudgery.

I am not naïve enough to believe that the world is full of "mute inglorious Miltons," but there are thousands upon thousands of buried talents that never come to light, and innumerable square pegs trying to distort themselves to fit into round holes, often for a lifetime.

What young people need to learn is that while it is not necessary to do better than others in your field, it is imperative that you can do better than those outside it. Only this provides a permanent edge in one's chosen occupation.

You can be an average doctor or an average plumber or an average anything in between — as long as you are more proficient than those who have no doctoring or plumbing skills. You are not ultimately competing against your peers; you are providing a service only a minority are qualified to undertake.

If a writer, for instance, compared himself with Shakespeare or Cervantes or Montaigne, he would never put pen to paper. But if he has even a smidgen of ability more than a nonwriter, and if he enjoys the craft, then he will make the most of his talent, small or large though it may be. Not everyone can write epics; somebody, after all, has to compose the ads and create the TV scripts.

Our doctrine of "individualism" has given us a false sense of competitiveness. What we are supposed to compete against is our own prior limits, just as a runner is competing not against other runners, but against his own previous best time. The others are there to spur him on, to test his limits, but he is really running against the clock, not against other humans.

By finding out what you do best, and by being the best you can at it, you will achieve a satisfaction that falls to too few — and never to those who are trying to beat others at their own game. The race indeed is not to the swift, nor the battle to the strong, but triumph comes to those who, every day and every year, get better at what they do.

When the Acorn Becomes a Maple

WHILE IT IS UNDOUBTEDLY TRUE that every acorn that grows up becomes an oak tree and not a maple or an elm, the same is obviously not true about human beings. There is no way of knowing or telling which kind of "tree" the seed is going to become.

With all our modern knowledge of genetics and psychology and education, nobody can predict how a baby will turn out, what kind of adult he or she will develop into. There are simply too many variables, too many contributing factors that we are still ignorant of.

We know a few negative things — that abuse or neglect or acute deprivation will scar or cripple forever the budding personality. But we have no positive formula for success in child-rearing: You do your best and you take your chances. Sometimes you win and sometimes you lose — and sometimes you are dead before the final score is posted.

Great men do not usually have great children; the genetic code does not operate that simply. Bright children come out of dull families, and vice versa. The successful executive is disappointed because his daughter wants to be a potter; the intellectual wonders why his son cares for nothing but cars and athletics. And all parents are astonished at the ways in which their offspring differ.

Almost from birth, it seems, products of the same genes will display widely diverse temperaments, aptitudes, interests, responses, and deficiencies. Nor does it seem to matter much how they are treated — these same faculties persist throughout a lifetime; they may be modified by training or experience, but they are not basically transformed.

It seems to me that parents would save themselves a lot of unnecessary grief (and their children a lot of unproductive guilt) if they simply accepted these diversities, these limitations, these inherent traits and tendencies. While it may be true that a child is the product of his environment, it is equally true that much the same environment will result in widely different products.

There is nothing approximating "quality control" in the natal system. By manipulating DNA in test tubes or other devices, we may be able to manufacture healthier human beings, but not wiser ones or more virtuous ones, which is what the world most needs.

Character is the all-important element in human conduct, and not even the greatest minds have been able to inform us how that can be transmitted. Socrates' most devoted pupil, Alcibiades, turned out to be a rotter. The son of an itinerant workman and an illegitimate mother who died when he was nine became our greatest president.

A professor in a business course, lecturing to his students, explained the difference between "education" and "experience" thus: "In reading a contract, education is what you get from reading the small print; experience is what you get from not reading it."

Money Is Time

I HAVE ALWAYS DISLIKED the phrase "Time is money." That is the least thing that time is, for it is irreplaceable, and not all the money in the world can bring it back, or halt it, or reverse it.

Actually, time is love. People who are always in a hurry, who have no time for anything except the most important matters, fail to understand the nature and the needs of love. Many a man in our society imagines that he is "supporting" his family by working long hours, attending innumerable meetings, and traveling incessantly. But though his motives may be good, his reasoning is faulty.

No amount of material goods can serve as an effective substitute for time spent with loved ones. The most "neglected" children are not necessarily those of the poor, but of the rich — or those trying to get there. There are no presents as important as presence.

We have become the victims of time. Our schedules are running us, instead of our running them. While it is true that people in the Middle Ages worked many longer hours than we do, a third of the days in a year were devoted to holidays, when the families were together.

Time is love in other ways as well — the time we spend with the old, the infirm, the time a doctor spends with a patient, the time a teacher spends with a student in special need of help, the time a pastor devotes to the personal problems of his flock. In all these areas, all of us are guilty of being dominated by the clock, of rationing our time so that everyone is "taken care of," but no one is really cared for.

Children, of course, are the most injured by our obsessive delusion that time is money. Fathers will spend weeks alienated from their children, and then imagine that an afternoon's fishing expedition or trip to the zoo makes up for this neglect.

It would be more realistic to turn the proverb around and

say that "money is time" — that the best thing money can do for you is to buy the time to demonstrate your love with your presence, your interest, your concern, and your pleasure.

Of course, I recognize that there are millions of broken families where this is hard, or impossible; and that millions of mothers with young children must work in order to meet the family's bills. But I wonder how many of these might still be together if the father had not put his job before his parental responsibilities, if the mother had not gone to work for reasons other than financial need.

Time is love, above all else. It is the most precious commodity in the world and should be lavished on those we care most about. When it is not, retribution is swift and certain and there is no turning back the clock.

Admitting Weakness Is a Strength

ALTHOUGH THE LATE President de Gaulle of France was generally considered to be a proud and even arrogant man, he was a shrewd enough psychologist to know when to discard this attitude. As Malcolm Muggeridge describes one public incident:

"I saw him on the French television being asked why he had delayed releasing the Ben Barka story till after the presidential election. Instead of getting hot under the collar, he just hung his battered old head sheepishly, and muttered in a woeful, strangled voice: *'C'etait mon inexperience.'* " ("It was my inexperience.")

The willingness to admit ignorance, or inexperience, which is much the same thing, is often an endearing trait, and it is surprising how, in so many cases, our pride and vanity inhibit us from the frank admission that we do not know.

Another great man, Sir William Osler, would make the grand rounds of a hospital, followed by a troop of admiring acolytes. Sometimes he would stop at a bed, examine a patient, and then scribble on the chart the initials "G.O.K." Later, one of the students made bold enough to ask the distinguished physician what "G.O.K." stood for. Osler, with a smile and a shrug, replied, "God Only Knows."

I was reminded of this story when a doctor mentioned the other night that one of his biggest problems in a teaching hospital is to get the interns and residents to admit that they are baffled by some symptoms.

"They seem to feel it is a reflection on their expensive medical education if they can't immediately apply their book learning to some cases," he said. "The most serious blunders, of course, are made by those who refuse to confess their limitations or lack of experience."

In his autobiography, Sir Cedric Hardwicke recounts the most moving moment he had ever witnessed in the theater. It was watching Ellen Terry when she was close to eighty, playing in the trial scene in *The Merchant of Venice*. As she approached Portia's "quality of mercy" speech, her face suddenly went blank. She struggled vainly for a moment and then moved down to the footlights.

"I am a very silly old lady," she said, "and I cannot remember what I have to say." Almost unanimously, Hardwicke recalls, the audience shouted the familiar lines and cheered as she smiled her thanks and returned to her place. She played out the rest of the scene to an enthralled audience.

It is our strength that may attract people to us initially, but it is our weakness that makes them like us, that touches some of their own inadequacies and forges a common bond of humanity. It is this one touch of nature that makes the whole world kin.

Education does not make us smarter, it merely propels us further and faster in the direction of our native abilities; and if one's ability is to make a fool of himself, education can help him do a magnificent job of that.

The Riper Pleasures of Old Age

As ONE GROWS OLDER, pleasures do not so much diminish as they change; one might say they move from the positive pleasures to the negative ones — from the youthful pleasure of looking forward to a party, to the riper pleasure of declining the invitation.

Anatole France once remarked that the chief benefit of being elected to the French Academy — the "Forty Immortals" — was that while he still had to make an appearance at the opening night of the opera, his new eminence permitted him to wear his bedroom slippers there.

When young, we are disconsolate if nothing good is happening to us, or promising to happen; in later age, we feel pleased merely if nothing bad is happening, or threatening to happen. "No news is good news" is a maxim that must have been devised by an older person.

This is what I mean by a negative pleasure: not the anticipation of a rainbow, but the avoidance of a thunderstorm; not of gaining something, but of retaining; not of being chosen, but of being spared. And one of the quiet delights is reading the obituary notices each morning and not seeing your name there.

There is also the satisfaction of not having to strive upward and onward; you are already everything you are going to be, no longer reaching out frantically for brass rings. And you are already who you are; no more searching for identity or status or whatever fickle fame teases and tantalizes us with in our early years.

One of the great negative pleasures is no longer having to prove yourself, to yourself or to others, either professionally or socially or sexually or in any other way. Competition may be stimulating when we are young, but exhausting and decreasingly rewarding as we get older. This gives us more energy, time, and sympathy (or should) to devote to the efforts of others less fortunate than we were.

Some older men retire to a farm; others keep working until the day they die. Either can help you live longer, depending upon your temperament and the needs of your body and your mind. What is important, in both cases, is learning to accept and enjoy the negative pleasures as keenly as we sought the positive ones when young.

Each new age is an apprenticeship; we must learn how to live it appropriately, how to find and hold its own kernel of gratification. I feel sorry not for old people, but for those who stubbornly seek to rekindle a lost youth, and even more for those who, glumly failing in this, refuse to make the most of what time is left to them.

People Are Hard to Change

THERE ARE SOME THINGS you can help change in people, and some things you can't. There are some things people can change in themselves, and there are some things they can't. Part of the wisdom of learning to live with others is knowing what can be changed and what cannot be, in oneself as well as in others. Some people never learn it: They spend their lives lowering buckets into wells and expecting to bring up wine.

You can change character, a little, by example or persuasion, but not by precept or authority. You can change temperament, very little, but only by tact and affection, never by criticism or scolding or nagging. You can change habits, but only with much difficulty and only if they were not formed in childhood as a reaction to an unpleasant environment. And, finally, it is far easier to change something about yourself than to change another.

All these may be psychological truisms, but it is surprising and dismaying how many persons torture themselves in trying to change someone who does not feel the need to be changed, who does not want to change, and who actually fears or resents what change might do to him or her. Someone, let us say, drinks too much because of low self-esteem. Drinking gives him or her a sense of confidence, even of ebullience. You cannot deprive that person of the liquor unless you provide the self-esteem. Someone else is habitually late. This is partly a matter of temperament, and partly a pattern of childhood experiences too complex for an easy analysis. Tardiness can mean any number of things; it can also mean simply that some people have an inherently defective sense of time. If this is so, no regimen or discipline on earth will do much good. You have to live with it or adapt to it as best you can.

I make these elementary points because I see all around me people struggling with their mates or wrangling with their children about traits and habits and dispositions that can never be changed with the methods they are using, and may never be changed at all by any methods yet known to mankind. In these struggles there is no communication — only fixed attitudes and accusations and anger, all of which are counterproductive. And the basic problem is that the accusers have never sorted out the things that can be changed from the things that cannot. It seems so clear to them that there is a right way and a wrong way to do everything, and the refusal to do those things their way is viewed as perversity, not incapacity.

I am far from suggesting, God knows, that the excessive drinker cannot change or be helped to change. But first he or she must want to. It must be through collaboration, not coercion, through compassion, not contempt. "I yam what I yam," as Popeye was fond of declaring, and while most of us can become a little more than we were and a little better than we were, few of us can become other than we are.

Why do so many people find it is easier to change the world than to change their minds?

Confusing "Character" with "Temperament"

TWO OF THE WORDS that we use about people I think we tend to use carelessly, and often interchangeably. These words are *character* and *temperament*.

As we grow older, we should learn that these are two quite different things. Character is something you forge for yourself; temperament is something you are born with and can only slightly modify. Some people have easy temperaments and weak characters; others have difficult temperaments and strong characters.

We are all prone to confuse the two in assessing people we associate with. Those with easy temperaments and weak characters are more likable than admirable; those with difficult temperaments and strong characters are more admirable than likable.

Of course, the optimum for a person is to possess both an easy temperament and a strong character, but this is a rare combination, and few of us are that lucky. The people who get things done tend to be prickly, and the people we enjoy being with tend to be accepting, and there seems to be no way to get around this. Obviously, there are many combinations of character and temperament, in varying degrees, so that this is only a rough generalization — but I think it is one worth remembering when we make personal judgments.

The core in the mystery of what we call personality resides in the individual mix between character and temperament. The most successful personalities are those who achieve the best balance between the strict demands of character and the lenient tolerance of temperament. This balance is the supreme test of genuine leadership, separating the savior from the fanatic.

The human Jesus is, to my mind, the ultimate paradigm of

such psychic equilibrium. He was absolutely hard on himself and absolutely tender toward others. He maintained the highest criteria of conduct for himself but was not priggish or censorious or self-righteous about those who were weaker and frailer. Most persons of strength cannot accept or tolerate weakness in others. They are blind to the virtues they do not possess themselves and are fiercely judgmental on one scale of values alone. Jesus was unique, even among religious leaders, in combining the utmost of principle with the utmost of compassion for those unable to meet his standards.

We need to understand temperament better than we do and to recognize its symbiotic relationship to character. There are some things people can do to change and some things they cannot do — character can be *formed,* but temperament is *given.* And the strong who cannot bend are just as much to be pitied as the weak who cannot be firm.

Old People Feel Young Inside

WHAT YOUNG PEOPLE fail to recognize until they themselves reach ripeness is that older people continue to regard themselves as young "inside" at any age, until death overtakes them. No matter how they may look or sound or even act, a core deep in themselves clings to the feeling that they remain perpetually young.

"Old age," said Bernard Baruch at eighty, "is always fifteen years older than you are." This sentiment has been echoed by many octogenarians. A part of ourselves — and a central part, it seems — remains boyish or girlish to the self-image we persist in holding to the very end.

Nearly everyone finds it hard to believe he or she has reached a certain milestone in life, be it fifty, sixty, or seventy; and no one (except perhaps the critically ill) feels internally that he is really that old. The cliché that "time flies" becomes truer every decade, and just that much harder to accept.

It is more incomprehensible now than it ever was before in human life, because not only are more people living longer, but they are living *younger:* that is, Americans today at sixty generally look and feel and behave no older than their parents did at forty. Just as our youngsters mature earlier, our oldsters age later, both in a physical and a social sense.

When I see a "grandmother" depicted in a television commercial, I am usually tempted to laugh at the outmoded stereotype of the gray-haired, bespectacled little lady spooning food to her grandchildren in the high-chair. Most of the women I know who have small grandchildren could almost pass as their mothers as easily as their grannies.

The tempo of life has so changed in the last generation or two — at least in the Western world — that most of the traditional roles and postures have lost their validity, and we require a new conceptualization of what Shakespeare depicted as "the ages of man."

No doubt people always felt much younger "inside" than they appeared to be; nowadays, the appearance conforms more nearly to the inner vision. Their diet, their exercise, their whole way of life, remove them from the sidelines to the mainstream of social and physical activity.

The official retirement age, once pegged at sixty-five, is now legally set at seventy. I predict that within a decade or so it will be lifted to seventy-five. The slogan of "equal opportunity" has become as much the banner of age as of race or sex. Older people used to ask for respect; now they demand to be judged by their vigor, not by the vicissitudes of time.

There is a distinct, if subtle, difference between the cynic and the skeptic: Confronted with something that seems too good to be true, the cynic doubts that it is good, while the skeptic doubts that it is true.

Climbing the Mountain of Success

IT HAS LONG STRUCK ME that the familiar metaphor of "climbing the ladder" for describing the ascent to success or fulfillment in any field is inappropriate and misleading. There are no ladders that lead to success, although there may be some escalators for those lucky enough to follow in a family's fortunes.

A ladder proceeds vertically, rung by rung, with each rung evenly spaced, and with the whole apparatus leaning against a relatively flat and even surface. A child can climb a ladder as easily as an adult, and perhaps with a surer footing.

Making the ascent in one's vocation or profession is far less like ladder climbing than mountain climbing, and here the analogy is a very real one. Going up a mountain requires a variety of skills, and includes a diversity of dangers, that are in no way involved in mounting a ladder.

Young people starting out should be told this, both to dampen their expectations and to allay their disappointments. A mountain is rough and precipitous, with uncertain footing and a predictable number of falls and scrapes, and sometimes one has to take the long way around to reach the shortest distance.

One needs different tools and the knowledge and skill to use them most effectively — as well as knowing when not to employ them. Most of all, a peculiar combination of daring and prudence is called for, which not all persons possess.

The art of rappelling is important, because sometimes one has to go down a little in order to go up. And the higher one gets, the greater the risk and the greater the fall; there is much exhilaration — but little security and less oxygen — in altitude. As many stars and standouts and company presidents have found to their regret, it is often harder to stay there than to get there.

Then, too, one must learn that there is no necessary relationship between public success and private satisfaction. The top of the ladder is shaky unless the base is firmly implanted and the whole structure is well defended against the winds of envy and greed and duplicity and the demands of one's own ego. The peak of the mountain is even more exposed to a chilling wind, as well as to a pervasive sense of loneliness. Many may have admired the ascent, but many more, eager to make the same endeavor, are waiting at the foot of the slope to witness an ignominious fall. It is easier to extend good will to those who do not threaten our own sense of worth.

People who are not prepared for failure are not prepared for success; if not for failure, at least for setbacks and slides and frustrations, and the acceptance of the deficits that so often accompany the assets. Ambition untempered by realism will never see the missing rung it falls through on that mythical ladder.

A Competitor's Most Dangerous Opponent

SOME YEARS AGO, a writer for *The New Yorker* magazine did a series on tennis, called "Levels of the Game," which vividly demonstrated that the game being played by champions on the court is not the same game being watched by the spectators. This is true, of course, in far more sports than tennis: What the spectator sees and appreciates is merely the overt action; what the expert is performing is an exercise in strategy at a far higher level that is as much psychological as it is physical.

I thought of this in reading about the chess championship match between Karpov and Korchnoi. For there are two games called chess, really — one is the game that persists in the public imagination and the other is the game that is actually played by masters over the board. The first game is tedious, abstruse, and mathematical, presided over by Olympian graybeards with prodigious memories, infinite patience, and the uncanny ability to project a dozen moves ahead. As it happens, none of these characterizations is correct: The best chess players are young, they don't all have good memories or mathematical prowess, and most of them can see only two or three moves ahead.

At its highest levels, chess, like all good games, whether tennis or bridge or poker, is psychological combat. All the top tennis players have roughly the same gifts of stroke production; all the leading card players are equally proficient in technique; all the tournament chess players know every opening, gambit, trap, and all their variations. It is the boldness, the imagination, the endurance, the playing on nerves, that eventually decide the contest. The essential personal factors of character and temperament make the ultimate difference between two combatants brandishing identical weapons.

The level of masters is beyond technique, aiming to exploit a personal weakness more than a technical defect: to move the opponent into an area where his self-confidence crumbles and his particular flaw is exposed to relentless attack. This flaw may be vanity or timidity or rashness or anger or arrogance — but it is always, at this level, a psychological weakness.

And this is what Smyslov, an earlier world's champion, alluded to when replying to an interviewer's question, "Who is your most dangerous opponent?" He said: "In chess, as in life, a man is his own most dangerous opponent." For, in every contest, more points and more games are lost by the loser than are won by the victor.

Uncertainty makes us so uneasy that we would rather have assurances that the worst is going to happen than remain long suspended in doubt — and sometimes we even precipitate the worst in order to relieve this anxiety.

Are You Retiring "From" or "To"?

A LOT OF WORDS have been written and said about the question of retirement, and most of them are unconvincing and inconclusive because they leave out the most important preposition in the proposition: That preposition is either *from* or *to*. Is a person retiring *from* something or *to* something — this is the significant aspect of the whole problem, and it is rarely confronted honestly and head-on.

If one is simply retiring *from* a job or position, one has to have something else in view that holds as much interest and attraction, or else nothing but boredom, triviality, and deterioration awaits the retiree.

If one is retiring *to* something — even a captivating hobby or long-delayed travel plans or catching up on years of neglected reading — then the retirement has point and purpose, and the machinery will be recharged and not simply run down.

Many men tend to slump over and die shortly after retirement, because they have retired *from* a challenging job and have found nothing to retire *to*. Their primary interest is not engaged in anything else, whereas even an ardent bird watcher or an engrossed stamp collector can be revitalized by an intense hobby that would bore another retiree to tears.

The chief danger and delusion in retirement, for many men, is imagining that they would like to spend the remainder of their years in playing golf or fishing or some other amiable pursuit — and then it turns out that these were really much more fun when one could slope off from work for a few days or weeks.

It is the intensity of interest, not the relaxation, that gives focus and stability to a retirement program. If you have been active all your life, and there is nothing you particularly want to do after retirement, or do on a regular basis, then the prognosis for contentment is not very good, and you will probably make your wife as miserable as you are.

Personally, I have never been a hobbyist; so luckily for me, when and if I do retire, I will keep on doing what I always have — writing and reading and lecturing and teaching, as long as health holds out.

But for those who must make a clean break with their profession or occupation, it is both physically and mentally necessary that they switch to another track, and not shunt themselves to the siding of life.

Notice that I have said "men" throughout this piece — ignoring comparable problems that women may have with the same situation, now that some 40 percent of our female population consists of working women. And since they tend, on the whole, to outlive the males, the time has come to inquire about their needs just as seriously.

Trying Too Hard May Sabotage Goals

IF YOU HAVE EVER TRIED to cut a log with a saw for a piece of firewood, you have learned a lesson that too rarely is applied to other forms of endeavor. You quickly learn that if you press down too firmly with the saw, it will not cut the wood; indeed, press down hard enough and the saw will not move at all. What is required is a moderate touch, firm enough to bite into the wood, but easy enough to facilitate the movement of the tool. The development of touch is perhaps the most neglected aspect in any craft or pursuit or career.

Two biographies recently came across my desk: one dealing with the political life of Hubert Humphrey, and the other with the military life of General Mark Clark.

What struck me most, in leafing through these books, was that, despite the disparity in their careers, both men failed to realize their ultimate goals by "wielding the saw" too intensely for cutting the log of their ambition.

Humphrey wanted desperately to be president of the United States, and it was precisely this fervent drive that broke him on the wheel of Lyndon Johnson's cruel cunning.

General Clark just as zealously aspired to gaining command of the Fifth Army, in preference to his rival, General George Patton. And he "succeeded" in engineering this coup — with the result that General Omar Bradley was put in charge of the invasion of France, while Clark languished in Italy on a bitter diversionary campaign.

What we most aspire to is often not what is best for us, and if we try too hard to get it, we may be surprised and dismayed at the consequences. "There are two disappointments in life," wrote Oscar Wilde. "One is not getting what you want. The other is getting it." (Especially, he might have added, if we get it prematurely, by pressing when we should have lain back a little, like a runner who has nothing left for the stretch, or a boxer who exhausts himself too soon.)

What we call timing in any art is mostly a matter of touch. It involves patience, waiting for the right moment, a willingness to go with events rather than anticipate them and thus distort them. Without ambition, success may elude us; but raw ambition that will not allow itself to be tempered can be equally disastrous to fortune.

"Our beginnings never know our ends," said T. S. Eliot. Sometimes the seemingly worst things happen for the best, and the best for the worst. All we can know for sure is that when we force the saw, we are more likely to break the teeth than cut the log.

If you're afraid of being a bore, you're probably not one: the mark of the true bore is his (or her) total unawareness of that possibility.

We Remain Beginners All Our Lives

MY BIRTHDAY SLIPPED BY last week with a minimum of fuss, at my firm request. When you get past a certain age, you really don't want your birthday remembered except by your nearest relatives. You are just glad you made it through another year — unless, of course, it is something special, like your ninetieth, which few of us are able to celebrate.

The salient fact that is ignored by most people who ponder the question of aging is that we enter each new age as beginners, no matter whether it is adolescence or senescence. Each age of life calls for a new set of attitudes, a new perspective on oneself, and a more or less difficult adaptation to its special requirements.

A man going from middle to old age is just as inexperienced in coping with his new status as he was in moving from youth to full manhood. He knows no more about the capacities and limitations of being older than he did when his voice changed from soprano to baritone.

Wisdom in external matters is, or should be, a steady accretion; wisdom about oneself must regularly be reviewed and renewed, at each stage of life. The only thing we don't have to learn to be is a baby; after that, life is a constant adjustment to our changing role in the general scheme of things.

Some persons shift gears more easily than others. I have met men (and women, too, of course) who seem to have been frozen in puberty, and never really wanted to make it into adulthood; while others, at fifty, resented the thought of getting old and dressed and acted like their children, not realizing what a foolish impression they made.

At the other extreme, I have known young men who seemingly could not wait to get old — who were born wizened, as it were, and would not feel comfortable with themselves until they acquired a shell of dignity or whatever they associated with the mantle of age. They are just marking time until time catches up with them.

It is fashionable now to speak of midlife crisis, but I suspect that every chronological shifting of gears involves a crisis, whether noted or not by the psychological trend spotters. A lot depends on how a particular society or culture happens to view the proper role and status of people in each age-group.

Bertrand Russell once said that he had missed at both ends: "When I was young, old people were respected; now that I am old, young people are admired." Values and perceptions change from generation to generation, and we must learn to adapt to them, not blindly to resist or resent them. The learning process never ends; when it does, you might as well be dead.

The Test of Rationality

A PECULIAR PARADOX about the human mind and emotional system is this: The best test I know for deciding how sane and rational you are is whether you can hold two contradictory ideas at the same time. It is a paradox because it seems irrational to hold two contradictory notions at the same time; but being able to do so indicates that you have the strength and sanity to withstand the tension between the two.

To take the most obvious example, what is your opinion about people generally? Is it that "People are no damn good" or that "People are on the whole splendid creatures"? If you adopt either viewpoint exclusively, I would suggest something is skewed in your perceptions of the world.

It seems clear to me that both statements are true, at different times, for different reasons, and often for the same persons. The contradictions are correct because people are really bundles of contradictions — just as light behaves sometimes as a "wave" and sometimes as a "corpuscle."

A person may respond like a hero to one crisis and like a coward in another; he may be generous in one area, or context, and selfish in another. Even those we designate as "saints" are not all of a piece; some have extremely unattractive aspects to their personalities.

Almost all people are multidimensional — that is, like gems, they refract different shades and hues, depending upon the angle at which they are held to the light. If we judge them, it must be in the round and not on the basis of the particular facet in our view.

The human personality is not like a single instrument, say a flute or a trumpet, but more like a vast organ, capable of playing from the deepest to the highest notes, and from the sweetest melodies to the most crashing cacophony — depending upon which keys or pedals are being pressed or depressed.

All nature, indeed, is a vast aggregation of contradictories; as botanists are fond of saying, a weed is just a plant in the wrong place for us. A fox is a pest in one kind of terrain, and a helpful predator in another. A bee pollinates as well as it stings.

So it is, also, with our social systems and economic arrangements and even sexual relationships. None of them is in perfect balance; each requires something of the opposite in order to maintain a productive tension. If there is one universal law, it seems to be that of uniting contradictories.

If you hold to one theory alone — about people or anything else — you are in trouble, and you are making trouble, for now and for the imminent future.

Women understand men better than men understand women not because they possess any superior faculty of insight, but because every minority (which women still are, practically if not numerically) develops a sensitivity in understanding the dominant majority far more than the majority bothers to understand them.

True Justice Requires Love

IF YOU LOOK in the dictionary, you will find the word *justice* defined there. But it is practically a useless definition, because it does not help us to determine where justice resides in any particular situation. Indeed, nobody has ever defined *justice* to general satisfaction in individual cases; the greatest minds ranging down from Plato and Aristotle have failed to pin down this elusive abstraction.

The reason for this, I think, is that justice alone, or mere justice, is not possible without something added to it — and this extra something must be on the order of mercy, or magnanimity, or to put it more commonly, love.

Mere justice is what gives each person his or her own due. But what *is* one's "own due"? What is owed to us by the fact of being a person, with the same rights as other persons? And what is our obligation to others with the same rights?

You probably know how the expression *a baker's dozen* arose. In times past, bread was so important that bakers were summarily prosecuted for giving short weight. In order to escape punishment for careless mistakes, they took to putting thirteen rolls into a bag that called for a dozen. They provided a little more than was due to the purchaser.

We often are told that marriage must be a "50-50 affair" in order to work. That is, each partner must go halfway to meet the mutual obligations of a marriage. But this is patently not enough; marriage is not a court of law in which each party gets or gives exactly what is due to him or her. One does not stand on the midway line and say, "This is as far as I go."

To work over a long period, marriage must be at least a 60-40 affair *on both sides.* Each partner must be willing to give 60 percent, not just 50, to the family enterprise. There must be an "overlap" of obligations, so that if at one point or another, for one reason or another, one of the partners is not pulling his or her own weight, the other will take up the slack.

"Justice" as a crude measurement does not operate here, because it does not surpass itself when conditions demand it. And without this little extra step, justice fails in an emergency, precisely when it is most needed. If justice is no more than the letter of the law — whatever the law may be — it falls short of human need, no less in a country or a community than in a family.

Noble abstractions like *justice* and *liberty* and *equality* cannot be defined because each of them involves something more than what the word connotes in a dictionary. They imply not a cold mathematical formula of addition and subtraction, but a living commitment to put one more roll into the bag, to make sure the weight is a little over what the law requires.

The Hyphen Makes Important Connections

FOLLOWING A COLLEGE LECTURE not long ago, somebody in the audience asked me what I thought was the greatest single advance in human knowledge. I replied that it was the use of the hyphen.

Uneasy laughter rippled through the auditorium. They assumed I was jesting, or being perverse, but I was in deadly earnest. It is only through the hyphen that we come — when we do — to a genuine understanding of the way the world actually works.

Politics cannot be comprehended without economics, and vice versa. Sociology is largely meaningless without psychology. Chemistry and physics are indissolubly linked. Astronomy was reaching a dead end until it turned into astrophysics.

It is only in the twentieth century that we actively began to use the hyphen in our investigations of basic subjects. Until then, most disciplines were locked into their own specialized grids, each with its separate body of principles and formulas and laws.

It was the growing realization of the interconnectedness of things that led to the massive breakthroughs in knowledge, so that we have learned more in the past half-century than in all the centuries preceding it; and, moreover, we have acquired the tools for further and deeper exploration.

In genetics, this overlap was responsible for the discovery of the double helix and the pathway of replication; in medicine, it provided a bridge from organic to psychosomatic illness; even in mathematics, it fostered the birth and development of symbolic logic.

The frontiers of all sciences are now interfaced; one is connected by a hyphen to another, as it is in nature. The artificial division between one subject and another has been broken down permanently, and it is in the flux between the two that we are finding the answers to ancient puzzles and perplexities.

Even in religious studies, "form-criticism" and linguistics and cultural anthropology have converged to give us a clearer understanding of the Bible and the different ways it has been interpreted over the centuries. (Not to mention misinterpreted by some of its most fervent followers.)

The hyphen represents a new way of looking at all life, not in terms of fixed and separate entities, but as interwoven patterns, in a dynamic relationship. Nowadays, if you know only your own subject, you do not know your subject sufficiently, with the breadth required to place it properly within the total scheme of things.

When computers were first devised, experts thought they would provide us with insights into the workings of the mind; but the more we learn about these machines, the more we become convinced that there is no useful analogy between human mentation and mechanical "intelligence."

Family Teaches Tolerance

MOST OF US who have bred and reared multiple children usually recognize that brothers and sisters need have nothing in common except their parentage. Our offspring, from the same genetic sources, can be as different as though they came here from different planets. Most, if not all, families have noted this.

But generally we fail to draw the right inference from this salient fact that each of our children is wholly different from the others. We persist in the notion — or rather, the myth — that a family is or ought to be a nest of congeniality, a unit of harmony, a mutual admiration society in miniature.

A family, however, is constituted for precisely the opposite reason: It is usually a bundle of contradictions, of conflicting needs and contrasting goals. It is meant to show us not how the same kind of people can get along, but how wildly disparate natures and temperaments can learn to live together without assaulting each other.

"Home," said Robert Frost, "is where, when you come back, they have to take you in." This is precisely the point, and it is a point of return. Members of the family rarely see eye to eye on the way the world looks to them; but a family is less like a political party than a place of refuge to shut out the world from time to time.

In a large sense, a family is more like a training camp. It teaches young people — and sometimes parents, too, if they are wise — how to coexist with very different creatures who are bound together. It teaches, at the very least, tolerance, if not acceptance, of humans who are just as exasperating, just as irrational, just as vain or stubborn as we are, in their own inexplicable ways.

This is one reason, perhaps the main reason, that only children find it so much harder than others to get along in later life. They have not been to "training camp," as it were, have not been subjected to the give and take of sibling rivalry, have not learned to roll with the punch and to take the bitter with the sweet.

"All happy families are the same," Tolstoi begins his famous novel, and then goes on to write about an unhappy family, showing us in part that unhappiness springs not so much from differences of temperament or character as from the unwilling-ness to accept these differences, to let them be, even to encour-age them.

We pride ourselves on being a realistic age, but we are gross sentimentalists in our idealization of what family life should be like. Young people, in this respect, are more realistic than their parents, for they ask to be accepted on their own emotional terms, not on some preconceptions the parents had long before the children were born. It may be the family that prays to-gether that stays together, but it is more likely to be the family that does not impose this ritual upon the unwilling.

"Intelligence" Comes in Many Forms

WELL BEFORE the psychologists dug very deeply into the sub-ject, I expressed the strong conviction that there really is no such singular thing as "intelligence." There are plural "intelli-gences" of different kinds, and the possession of one kind does not necessarily imply another.

I would even extend this division to the faculty that is com-monly called "card sense," which some people are supposed to have and others not. I suspect even that is too broad a general-ization to be true. For instance, I consider myself to be a tolera-bly good poker player, but only a third-rate (if that) bridge player, even though I have played much more bridge than poker and take it far more seriously. Also, along those lines, as a young man I used to beat almost every checker opponent I came across, but although I labored diligently over the chess board, I have never been more than a *patzer*. Whatever shape of intelligence I may have does not conform to the patterning of bridge or chess.

The most dramatic example, I suppose, was Alexander Alekhine, the greatest chess master of our time. All the money he won at chess he promptly tossed back at the bridge table, under the fatal delusion that he was as skillful at the one as at the other. He died broke, from gambling as much as from drink.

The man who makes $10 million devising a new product surely has a different intelligence "bite" than the man who can build a beautiful period cabinet; and whatever kind of intelligence I may have, I am totally incapable of doing either. Without a slight gift for reasoning and writing, I could easily starve to death.

Everybody is dumb about different things and in different ways. Even a so-called polymath has intellectual powers that few possess, but he may be unable to tie his shoelaces correctly or cross a busy street in safety.

I am convinced that we were given diverse sorts of intelligence because no one kind alone could assure the preservation, much less the progress, of the human species. I could have lived two hundred years and never figured out how to build the first bridge over a stream — but the first bridge builder probably couldn't count past ten without taking off his shoes.

It's time we stopped using "intelligence" with a capital "I" and moved it down to its proper lower-case position. All you have to do is listen to a general for a few minutes to realize how limited Military Intelligence really is.

I've always been fond of Jean Cocteau's suggestion that the idea of "luck" was invented by man, because "how else can we explain the success of those we don't like?"

How Can Man Cast Out Fear?

IN A LIFETIME OF READING, one begins to realize how much has been written about love, and how little about hate. Yet hate is, in a sense, the greater force, in that it can destroy in a single moment what love has taken years to build.

It seems to me that we spend too much time sentimentalizing over love and too little effort to understand the roots and ramifications of hate, a destructive element far more rampant than any number of nuclear warheads.

This is true not merely in personal terms, but on a tribal or national scale as well. It took the Israelis many loving years to build up a prosperous and fertile country; it can take only a few hours or days to devastate the entire Middle East.

St. Paul informs us that perfect love casts out fear; but the reverse is equally, and more dreadfully, the case — fear drives out love and transforms it into a raging and implacable hatred.

The Palestinians fear extinction; the Israelis fear destruction; the Arab states fear revolt and revolution. Each position hardens out of fear, until conflict becomes inevitable, though all may desire a less devastating confrontation.

How do we deal with the mechanism of hate born of fear? The world has never really addressed itself to this basic problem. Disputes have been settled *ad hoc* around the conference table or on the battlefield — but each "settlement" contains the seed of renewal.

We speak of "love" as the ultimate solvent, but before love can come into operation, we have to find a way to reduce the mutual fear that feeds on itself and eventually consumes itself in warfare. We must learn how to tame and rechannel the torrent of hate that now, for the first time, has the capacity to obliterate most of mankind.

What is so tragically ironic today is that the only way governments feel they can adequately defend themselves is by playing on the fear of the "enemy" — as we are told to fear the Russians and they to fear us. Yet, on a personal level, I doubt that the average Russian family feels any more animus against our people than we do against theirs. But all are egged on by their regimes in order to justify the gigantic arms build-up.

Publics are manipulated psychologically for political purposes, we no less than the Soviets, the Israelis no less than the Palestinians, the British no less than the Argentinians. We respond to hate, because it thrives on prejudice and ignorance, whereas love calls for knowledge and understanding.

The most imperative thing needed in the world at this time is a community of nations, and it has never seemed further away. Perhaps it will take a holocaust of hate to burn the fear out of us and leave the saving remnant — if any — holding hands amid the ashes.

On Wanting to Be Many Things

I REMEMBER when one of my sons was still in puberty, he was asked that perennial question, "What do you want to be when you grow up?"

He reflected for a while, and then said, "I want to be a skin diver in the summer, a telephone lineman in spring and fall, and a scientist in the winter."

Amusing, I suppose, that a little boy wanted so many diverse vocational lives. Yet, in some way, there is both a physical and a psychological truth embodied in this childish dream that most of us have been forced to ignore or severely suppress in our adult lives.

Specialization is at the heart of our modern industrial and commercial society. As Adam Smith told us two centuries ago, it is specialization that makes progress possible, that brings prosperity, that oils the smoothly whirring wheels of civilization.

The cost of this, however, is often quite high, especially in terms of the adult male personality. For there are deep and permanent needs in our nature that cannot be satisfied by one kind of work — even by the kind of work we most enjoy doing and do best. A part of us remains submerged; usually, to make a bad pun, the skin diver part.

This is no doubt why so many men pursue their hobbies with fanatical devotion, from gardening to woodworking to hunting and fishing and tinkering with motors. The office, the factory, the laboratory, gratify only one aspect of the personality, if they gratify us at all. For a man is a generalist by nature, if a specialist by necessity.

It was not foolish for my son to have wanted these incompatible careers; it was merely impractical in our social and economic system. But any lad instinctively knows that his body requires the exercise the lineman gets, that his spirit needs the challenge facing the skin diver, even though his mind is attracted to the largely sedentary life of the scientist.

A large part of our urban discontent and crime and delinquency, I am persuaded, springs from the dwindling opportunity to release vital powers in the modern mechanized world, to make a decent living out of it, and to be respected for it — unless you happen to be a star athlete, which many men secretly (or openly) yearn to be.

Our overemphasis on sports and physical feats is a symbol of this sense of deprivation we feel, as we become more mechanized, more specialized, more urbanized, more confined to routine. Adam Smith feared it might turn us into robots; so far, it has only transformed us into joggers.

Americans are the only people I know who are instinctively suspicious of those who speak English in well-formed sentences, as if precision in speech were somehow a character flaw.

No One Likes a Tattletale

ONE OF THE MOST DIFFICULT moral problems for man lies in the area of what is loosely called "loyalty." We have not yet straightened out our priorities on what should be told, to whom, and under what circumstances.

From childhood on, our social mores condemn the "snitch" and the "tattletale." Group solidarity demands that nobody tell on the perpetrator of a misdeed or a piece of mischief. And, generally, the snitch is what kids call a "suck-up," seeking to ingratiate himself with the authorities.

But there is a larger sphere of morality than this in-group code. How large or grievous does the infraction have to be before someone will spill the beans? How dangerous or how long does a condition have to persist before somebody decides to blow the whistle?

What has been happening — in our society, at least — is that the ethos of keeping your mouth shut has taken precedence over the ethos of the general good, and it takes a skywalk collapse or a shuttle disaster before anyone will step forth to point at the probable culprit. By that time, of course, the damage has already been done, which might well have been avoided by a prior warning.

Although sometimes the whistle may be swallowed in order to protect one's job or even to win a promotion for maintaining a conspiratorial silence, more often it is simply the social opprobrium that attaches to the mere act of snitching on a colleague or an associate. In this respect, most of us remain children for a lifetime.

And the reason, as I suggest, is easy to understand. Among children, the tattletale is usually not animated by an abstract sense of high morality but by the thought of currying favoritism with the mighty. The child wants to win Brownie points at

the expense of his schoolmates, and is properly considered rep-
rehensible for this.

As we grow older, though, our sphere of loyalty is supposed
to expand, eventually to include the whole social order to
which we belong; if our loyalties remain parochial, we will tolerate almost any degree of evil rather than put the finger on
the malefactor in our midst. In this way, "respectable" society
adopts the code of gangland.

What makes this a knotty problem is that one has to be sure
one's motives are straight and pure and that one does not gain
personally by peaching on the infractor — and also, of course,
that the matter is serious enough to warrant the whistle. It is so
much easier to lie low and pretend to ourselves that our moral
cowardice is "loyalty."

Sincerity Can Be Dangerous

THE MOST DANGEROUS LIARS in the world, I have found, are
not the people who lie to other people, but the people who lie
to themselves.

I know a prominent politician who has never told a lie to the
populace that he did not first believe himself. This is why he
can convey it with such an air of total sincerity.

Of course, it depends upon how one defines a *lie*. Objec-
tively, it is a misstatement of fact. If the speaker believes it to
be true, is he uttering a lie or simply a misstatement?

Out of kindness, we may decline to call it a lie — but what if
the utterer has closed his mind, and refuses to reexamine the
fact? Is not the willingness to believe a lie as much a spiritual
and intellectual sin as consciously perpetrating a falsehood?

I believe it is, because the truly evil leaders of mankind have
not been the hypocrites and manipulators of public opinion,
but the impassioned zealots who are absolutely convinced that
what they are saying is the Gospel truth.

This is why, and how, they exercise such hypnotic influence

upon their followers. Many of Hitler's lieutenants may have been (and were) cynical about his rantings, but he himself never doubted for a moment that his paranoid delusions reflected reality in the outside world.

Most people seem to value "sincerity" as a virtue more than I do. But sincerity is not an independent virtue, like truth. If you are wrong, the more sincere you are, the more damage you can do, and the more wrong-minded followers you are able to attract.

What we call "charismatic" influence is generated by absolute sincerity, combined with singleness of purpose; and far more evil has been wrought by single-minded fanatics than by any number of cunning hypocrites.

The golden-tongued charmer eventually trips on his own duplicity; the "true believer" can go straight to his doom — as Hitler did — taking millions of gullible followers with him. Absolute and unshakable conviction has a hypnotic power that goes beyond rhetoric and far beyond reason.

Sly and devious leaders may do some damage to the commonwealth, but their influence is rarely fatal. It is when sincerity is divorced from rationality that we are led into the terrible wars and revolutions that destroy more than they preserve or reform.

All of us lie to ourselves, about one thing or another, far more than we lie to others. And it is when we are inextricably bound to these lies that we do the most harm, to ourselves and to all around us. Sincerity that thinks it is the sole possessor of the truth is a deadlier sin than hypocrisy, which knows better.

As long as there exists a capacity for shame, there exists a potential for goodness; and what is most alarming about modern society is not the extent of wickedness but the diminished sense of shame — from something as trivial as littering to as grave as perjury.

Princes and Presidents Need Good Critics

NEAR THE END, Dante had little to lose by being impertinent to the powers that be. Impoverished, exiled for almost twenty years, his philosophic book burned in public and placed on the Papal Index (where it remained for three hundred years), Italy's greatest poet could take no more.

When the Prince of Verona asked him how he could account for the fact that, in the household of princes, the court fool was in greater favor than the philosopher, he replied with reckless sarcasm:

"Similarity of minds, your Highness, is all over the world the source of friendship."

A rude and brutally candid remark to make to a man who could send you to your death; but Dante was beyond caring. What could be done to him that had not been done already? Everything was long ago lost, except his genius and his fierce independence.

And his retort was true enough, as the world goes. Presidents, no less than princes, gather around them men who not only share their opinions (which is understandable), but also live at much the same level of sensibility as they do. Men, in short, who make them feel comfortable with themselves, who do not raise embarrassing questions about motives or methods or goals.

This is one of the perennial problems of political leadership. Similarity of mind and tastes and background makes for easy relationships, but easy relationships make for difficult statesmanship; when all see the same way, nobody sees what ought to be seen.

In dictating his memoirs, Napoleon confessed his regret that he had quarreled with Talleyrand. "It was my big mistake," he said, "because he had things I needed, and I had things he needed." But Napoleon in his prime could brook no opposition; even in exile on Elba, nobody dared beat him at chess, and he gave up the game in boredom.

Princes and presidents, most of all, require advisers of a keener sensibility, of a critical nature, of an independent mind, to supply the qualities they may lack. But even Frederick the Great, patron of the arts and student of philosophy, could not bear to have Voltaire around for very long, like a pebble in his shoe.

The court fools were retained for a lifetime and often said in jest the painful truth that would assure the dismissal of the court philosopher. The fool provoked laughter; the philosopher only aroused resentment. This is the danger of "compatibility" in high places.

Few Contribute to Human Progress

THE MODERN MAN'S visual picture of the "Stone Age" consists mainly of a beetle-browed creature in a loinskin, brandishing a club in one hand and with the other dragging a woman by her hair into his cave.

Some years ago, I recall, a graduate class in anthropology at Berkeley was commissioned by the professor to make a stone tool, using the same tools as Stone Age people had.

The class spent nearly a whole semester on the project — and no one succeeded in making a stone tool of the same quality and usefulness as those made by the barely upright hominids of hundreds of thousands of years ago.

In any generation, only a few persons possess the minds, the skills, and the imagination to devise what we call "advancements" in human living. Given the paucity of knowledge and the scarcity of equipment, the inventiveness of the Stone Age was even more remarkable than our progress in the Electronic Age.

Not one out of a million among us makes any real difference, in this primary sense. Nor do we ever know where this one is coming from or exactly how he makes the leap to a new plateau.

We live mainly off the incomes — both intellectual and material — generated by a small genetic pool of geniuses, not by statesmen or generals or financiers, who simply utilize (or corrupt) the products of these rare minds for their own purposes. And we would be living today in much the same fashion as Stone Age man, were it not for these few men of vision and persistence and patience, who have rarely reaped personal rewards from their inestimable contributions to our knowledge.

The mass of modern population knows much more than our primeval ancestors did, but what we know makes little difference to the future; most of us live and die as though we had not been at all, in any basic evolutionary sense.

There is no reason to believe that we breed more geniuses per capita than the cavedwellers did. The quantum jumps in civilization — what the paleontologists properly call "Ages" — are made by a handful in any era, who are mankind's most precious commodity.

The most that the rest of us can do is to provide a setting and an atmosphere that is open and hospitable to the broadest stretch of creative thinking — and to hope that the fruits for our offspring will be sweet, not bitter.

Making Old Age a Mellow Time

I WAS PART OF A PANEL on a health program not long ago, and one of the questioners wanted to know why we spend so much money on cancer research in this country. "After all," he said, "cancer tends to be an older person's ailment, and we should devote more of our funds and energy to keeping younger people alive."

This is an insensitive attitude on several counts. It is true that more people are living longer, and therefore the incidence of cancer is bound to increase proportionally. But it is important to society that older people live out their years as free from pain and anxiety as possible. It is important because old age should be a time of relaxing, relinquishing, and reaching out. Optimally, it should be a time when the aged are able to show patience, tolerance, and acceptance of their changing sphere of influence. If older people are chronically suffering, it is hard for them to come to terms with their frailties, let alone with any grace or humor. Instead, they become more encrusted, more self-involved, more loath to let go of the reins and diminish the demands of their egos.

The whole point of aging is mellowing, broadening, a willingness to give instead of take, to participate without dominating. But this is difficult, if not impossible, when you are ravaged by a mortal ailment — and when you know, moreover, that it may be conquered or subdued only a few years after your death.

Anything that softens the passage of age tends to lubricate the whole social mechanism. It is the men and women who refuse to relax their grip who make it so hard for themselves and for those around them. For pain, while it weakens us physically, makes us more tenacious in hanging on to our perquisites and prerogatives.

Old age should be an unfolding, a yielding, an opening of the personality, not a shrinking, a hardening, or a cranky preoccupation with the self. We should grow more considerate, more contemplative, letting life stream past us without criticism or rancor or resentment at fate. As Richter said, "Nothing is more beautiful than cheerfulness in an old face."

This attitude is hardly possible to one ravaged with illness, whose last years or months are shadowed by the specter of death. Anything we can do to ease, if not entirely obliterate, that shadow, lightens the spirit not only of the victims but of the whole human landscape across the generations.

Man's Success Lies in Versatility

THE GREAT STRENGTH of all other species lies in their *uniformity*. It is in humankind alone that the great strength lies in *diversity*. Until you understand this profound and radical difference, you cannot appreciate our absolute dependence upon differences among people.

The lion, the rabbit, the snail, and all the others each have one thing they do superbly well. This keeps them alive, both individually and as a species. But they cannot do other things, and, most of all, they cannot change and develop with a changing environment.

It is man's versatility, more than his brain power, that ensures his survival. We cannot fly as well as a bird, swim as well as a fish, run or climb or fight as well as other creatures — but we can do all of these in combination, using our tools.

If there were only one kind of person in the world — a hunter or a fisherman or a farmer — we would long ago have perished. But we have an infinite variety of mankind; thus, different types and different skills permit us to prevail in different ages and different crises.

And this is why all bigotry, all provincialism, all narrow pride in one's own "kind," is not merely morally objectionable — it is materially damaging. We need every kind of talent and viewpoint there is.

It is true in politics and social life as much as anywhere else. The conservative who would prefer all people to be conservative or the liberal who yearns for all men to see his way is dangerously shortsighted and self-destructive, for development thrives only on opposition.

No one can grasp the whole of truth. Each of us has partial vision. The conservative is blind without the liberal, just as the liberal is lame without the conservative, for each only touches a part of the elephant and not the whole creature. And every society needs its radicals, whether they are right or wrong, to question received opinions that may have become obsolete or obstructive to further development.

It is no biological accident that humans are more individuated than any other species. This is our salvation. Pluralism is not simply a pleasant doctrine of tolerance, of "live and let live." Rather, without pluralism we would not be able to live very long on this planet before being overwhelmed by one catastrophe or another.

Yet, it is also part of our nature to want other people to be more like us and to draw away from those who seem different. If the human race ever commits suicide it will be because one dominant strain has been able to wipe out all the others — and in so doing has assured its own extinction. What we call "tolerance" is not a moral luxury, but a vital imperative.

Information Is Useless Without Comprehension

WE ARE INFORMED, in a full-page ad by United Technologies, that personal computers are expected to turn up in four out of five American homes by 1990. In addition, "by linking a computer to a TV set and then to the telephone network and outside data banks, we will transform our homes into communications centers with access to an array of information services."

What troubles me in this glowing prospect is the overload of information without enough coherence or clarity to do more than confuse and confound the public even more than ever. It is not merely that we require more information today: We need more comprehension and more credibility. That is, we need to understand the thousands of bits of information that assault us daily, and we need to be able to believe the sources. What is the good of acquiring information if it comes so fast and so scrappily that we are unable to make much sense of it, and,

further, if we cannot tell whom or what to believe in this constant bombardment of presumed facts and dubious data? Both
our sensory and our intellectual apparatus can absorb only so
much before they begin to rebel.

Our imperative need today, it seems to me, is not for more
information as such, but for a framework into which we can
place the events we learn about, some schematic structure that
will allow us to make sense out of the thousands of discrete
chunks of data that are hurled at us every moment of our wak-
ing lives. Our information processes require more *depth* and
definition and *dimension* if we are to cope realistically with the
pace of change in modern society; but the more quantity we
get, the less quality there seems to be, and the more events we
hear about, the less we seem to grasp about each. If we get to
know less and less about more and more, eventually we shall
know nothing about everything.

The ad tells us that we are entering "a new information age,"
but the only thing new is the speed and accessibility with
which raw data enter our ears and eyes. But raw data are
meaningless, or even confusing, until we have been given the
tools for analyzing, evaluating, and digesting them — and neither our educational system nor our ancillary modes of communication have provided us with these necessary tools.

Computers can only assemble and distribute information.
They cannot do our thinking for us. And if our mental processes remain primitive, the more sophisticated our equipment,
the more baffled we become through our instruments.

Medicine Is an Art

I DO NOT WISH TO DENIGRATE or dispraise the technical mar-
vels of modern medicine, which no doubt have saved lives and
shortened terms of illness. Both diagnosis and therapy can use
all the help they can get, by whatever means available. Yet I

cannot help wondering how much of this new equipment is a *supplement* to the doctor's craft, and how much is becoming simply a *substitute* for it. For I do not think there can ever be an adequate substitute for the healing art. In this I am not merely expressing an uninformed layman's opinion. In his book *Letters to a Young Surgeon,* Dr. Richard Selzer (author of the highly acclaimed *Mortal Lessons*) begins by cautioning the medical student:

> Do not rely upon the X-ray machine, the electrocardiograph, or the laboratory to tell you what your hands and eyes and ears can find out, lest your senses atrophy from disuse. The machine does not exist that can take the place of the divining physician. The physical examination affords the opportunity to touch the patient. . . . In this exchange, messages are sent out from one to the other that, if your examination is performed with honesty and humility, will cause the divining powers of the Augurs to be passed on to you.

Poetical as this may sound, I believe it also to be the truth. Communication is the most important element between patient and doctor, and this communication must be more than verbal — it must involve all the senses, brought to concert pitch by intensive medical training that no machinery can provide.

There is a double danger involved here: not merely that the physician will become too reliant upon the instrument and the laboratory, but also that this increasing dependence may distance him from the patient as a person. Hardly any relationship is as personal as that between the healer and the hurt; when that diminishes, or is lost, some essential thread is snapped in the therapeutic process.

Scientific gadgetry can no doubt accomplish a great deal that could not be done without it; every hospital is eager to buy the latest and largest device it can afford, and some it cannot afford, for reasons of prestige as much as for practice. The seduction of technology, however, poses as much a threat as a promise to the ancient and honorable art of medicine.

This is no nostalgic call for a return to the horse-and-buggy days, when a doctor's little black bag contained little that could harm you, and just as little that could help you. It is, however, a reminder that though we can now place a heart in a human being, we will never be able to install a heart in a hunk of steel.

Life's Unfairness Is No Excuse for Human Injustice

WHEN AN UNDERLING COMPLAINED that something was "unfair" in the White House setup, Jack Kennedy is reported to have snapped back at him, "Life is unfair!"

This piece of stoical philosophy is supposed to help us bite the bullet and accept the injustices that come our way. I happen to look upon it quite differently.

Life, of course, *is* unfair. Misfortune can happen to anyone at any time, from an assassination to an avalanche. Nature is, if not hostile, at least indifferent to our fates; when a plane crashes, the innocent perish along with the guilty.

But this is all the more reason for us to strive for as much fairness as possible in *human* relations. Since we are the pawns of fate, or accident, in a naturalistic sense, we ought to do everything in our power to support and safeguard one another in a humanistic sense.

We should not add our own unfairness to the glacial indifference of the cosmos. We should not impose additional barriers or handicaps upon our own species, but rather join in a collective effort to make the globe a little safer, a little more secure. It is precisely *because* life is so capricious in its nonhuman aspects that we have an obligation to inject as much fairness and decency as we can into our relationships, whether they be social or economic or marital or parental. There is enough undeserved agony in the world without our adding to it by personal unfairness, either actively or by our passive acquiescence in injustice to another.

This is not sentimentalism; it is simply good sense. John Donne's declaration that "no man is an island" is not a religious incantation; it is a social and biological imperative on this tiny spaceship we call the earth, whirling through the cosmos to a problematic future.

It is both glorious and perilous to be alive. Joys and delights, sorrows and misfortunes, lurk around every corner. Our great enemy is time and the unknown, yet we expend most of our energy in fighting one another, rather than in banding against our common foe.

The essential unfairness of life, the vast impersonality of nature, is a condition to be resisted and rectified as much as possible, not to be accepted with a fatalistic shrug and compounded by our own contribution to conflict.

If by our efforts, singly and collectively, we cannot make life fairer — in those elements that are within human control — what meaning and what value can we find to justify man's "brief authority" upon this petty planet?

A great sorrow either deepens us or drains us: It makes the learning person more compassionate and resilient, and the obdurate person more bitter and banal.

■

It is not the optimist who thinks this is the best of all possible worlds but the pessimist; the optimist always hopes it can be made better.

Dividing the World in Half

ONE QUOTATION that I have cherished perhaps more than any other over the years came from Irwin Edman long ago, when he was still teaching at Columbia. He said: "The world is divided into two kinds of people — those who divide the world into two kinds of people, and those who don't."

Quite apart from the self-reflexive wit of this remark, it is perfectly true that almost all of us are guilty of this mental and moral sin — of dividing humanity into Our Sort and Their Sort.

The divisions can be of any kind — racial, religious, national, sexual, social, intellectual, political. Even invalids tend to divide the world into sick people and well people. Young people, of course, are said to regard the over-thirty class as The Other, if not as The Enemy.

And villagers likewise skew the population into Country Folk and City People, as if each were a homogeneous group, one possessing all the homely virtues, and the other a cesspool of vices.

Only a minority — a small minority — in every age has refused to make these divisions. Only a few take people where and how they find them, judging them not by some particular or parochial standard, but by a broader human measurement that encompasses the whole species of mankind.

This is what Edman meant by the second group, to which he belonged. In every era known to history, it has been a small group, and it does not seem to be growing larger, despite the fact that the world is getting smaller.

There seems to be some primordial need in the human animal to identify with a group that represents a subspecies, even though we are biologically one kind. A psychological drive, as yet unidentified, seems to compel us to divide rather than unite — even though, in this era, we are painfully aware that all of mankind is on the same tiny spaceship whirling like a speck of dust throughout an infinite cosmos.

Somehow this is too much for our imagination to grasp or to accept, and so we retreat into more comfortable assumptions of identity. We define ourselves by partial allegiances that soon become predominant. Only a few hundred years ago, there was no such thing as a "Frenchman" or an "Italian," except in a broad geographical sense; today, millions will fight and die for such nationalistic abstractions.

Man cannot give up one identity (the "Breton" or the "Venetian") without adopting another. He needs something larger than himself, but less than the whole, to feel a part of. It is this seductive and treacherous trait that may in the end prove our undoing and doom us to extinction as a species.

If couples get married for trivial reasons, why is it not to be expected that they will get divorced for trivial reasons?

■

People who are proud of doing their duty rarely suspect that the sin of pride cancels out the virtue of duty.

■

The ongoing "revolution" in sexual conduct was predicted long ago by those who warned that a moral code based largely on fear would disintegrate when and if the fear was ever removed.

■

Why do we expect people to be "happy" after marriage who were never happy before it?

■

Those who are first to applaud are generally last to understand what they are applauding.

PART IV

——

OF THE
FINE AND VULGAR
ARTS

Society Appreciates Geniuses Centuries Late

EACH GENERATION IMAGINES that it is more "enlightened" than the previous one. Superficially, this may be so; but at a deeper and more permanent level, attitudes and tastes change far more slowly than we think they do.

Most of the audience who viewed the film *Amadeus,* portraying the brief and frustrating life of Mozart, left the theater deploring the way he was treated in his time, especially the lack of appreciation and patronage in his native land. We suppose it would be different today — that we would take Mozart to our hearts, and gratefully accord him the honors and emoluments we reserve for our rock stars and film luminaries.

There is no reason to harbor this conceit. Serious composers — as well as serious creators in other artistic realms — fared comparatively better in the age of patrons, whether they were archdukes or archbishops, than in the modern world, with very few exceptions.

In his perceptive biography of Mozart's life and works, written nearly fifty years ago in England, the splendid critic W. T. Turner made this observation in a footnote:

Since Mozart's day, artists have exchanged the patronage and official employment of the heads of States, Churches, and people in authority for the "freedom" to work competitively in the market.

For a time this worked tolerably well, but with the twentieth century and universal education, the artist found that he was now at the mercy of the lowest common taste of the multitude. Mozart's situation today would be even worse than in 1777.

In those days, the Emperor Joseph could complain to Mozart, at the conclusion of one of his concerts, that his music contained "too many notes." The composer demurred. "I think not, Your Highness," he said. "There are exactly the number that are needed."

Today, he would be heard by only a handful, and barely supported, while tens of millions were swelling the coffers of a Neil Diamond or a Stevie Wonder or some comparable contriver of banal tunes. Mozart was rejected in Vienna by precisely the same popular audience.

The arts cannot be self-supporting because it usually takes decades, and sometimes centuries, for the populace to catch up with its true geniuses, whether they be Mozart dumped into a pauper's grave in the eighteenth century, or Bartók dying in a charity ward in the twentieth.

Please Explain Your Play, Mr. Pinter

IN HIS DIVERTING BOOK *Undying Passion,* a collection of letters from one sex to the other, Joseph Orgel quotes Harold Pinter's reply to a lady correspondent who wrote to his home in London:

> "I would be much obliged if you would kindly explain to me the meaning of your play *The Birthday Party*. These are the points I do not understand: 1. Who are the two men? 2. Where did Stanley come from? 3. Were they all supposed to be normal?
>
> "You will appreciate that without the answers to these questions I cannot fully understand your play."

To which Pinter promptly replied:

"Dear Madam: I would be obliged if you would kindly explain to me the meaning of your letter. These are the points I do not understand: 1. Who are you? 2. Where do you come from? 3. Are you supposed to be normal?

"You will understand that without the answers to my questions, I cannot fully understand your letter."

You may consider Pinter's reply pert or impertinent, as you will, but he is really "answering" her questions by implication, and suggesting how a serious play — or any creative literature — should be viewed.

Does the lady correspondent know who she is? Precisely why she married the man she did, or why she stays with him? Why her children are what they are, and why each one is so different? Does she know what a "normal" person is, and why so many "normal" persons seem to do abnormal things?

"Our beginnings never know our ends," says T. S. Eliot, and most consequential drama is about our tangled beginnings and our obscure ends. It does not answer any of the questions the lady asks — it poses them more pregnantly and compels us to reflect more honestly and deeply upon the mysterious processes of personality.

Only shallow television plays have straightforward plots and endings that are neatly tied up in the last five minutes before the commercial. A play that "makes a point," in this sense, need not have been written, except as light entertainment, or a didactic lesson pretending to be genuine drama.

A play of consequence cannot solve our perplexities, but hopes to illuminate them, to act as a kind of laser beam cutting beneath the skin and bone, to the core of our carefully concealed sensibility. The author may understand his characters better than we do, but they do not understand themselves; if they did, they would be larger than human. And if they did, there would be no drama, only a lecture. This, after all, is the difference between *Hamlet* and a case study.

Great Music Is Forever New

SOME MONTHS AGO, I used the phrase *great music* and several people asked how I would define it. The best definition of *great music* I have ever heard came from Artur Schnabel, the eminent concert pianist, who said: "Great music is music that is written better than it can be played."

This is why popular songs, no matter how beguiling or lovely they might be, cannot be classified as "great." It is not a matter of snobbery or tradition or even craftsmanship in composing, but something far deeper and difficult to put into words.

For an accomplished artist, it is easy to get out of a popular song everything the composer has put into it. But the most skilled musician in the world cannot exhaust the content of one of the late Beethoven piano sonatas, or a Mozart quartet.

No matter how faithfully he plays it, there is always something beyond that eludes the definitive interpretation. Schnabel himself spent a professional lifetime trying to capture the essence of what Beethoven wrote. He came as close as anyone, but not to his own satisfaction.

Moreover, each time the instrumentalist plays a piece of great music, he finds new meanings and nuances within, secrets that give themselves up only slowly and teasingly. However great his skill, he never succeeds in reproducing everything that was in the composer's intent. The ultimate performance of a great composition is as out of reach as the ultimate production of *Hamlet*.

"I never play the same piece twice in the same way," said Pablo Casals, the premier cellist of our time. "Each time it is new." He also confessed that he had studied the Bach suites for twelve years "before I had the courage to play one of them in public."

Except for a few old dance tunes that are kept alive through nostalgia, popular music changes every year or so. The ear becomes tired of listening, the tunes grow stale with familiarity, because the musical content is so thin and lacking in nourishment. We require, and demand, novelty because at bottom we remain unsatisfied.

In 1985 the world commemorated Bach's tercentenary. He was born three hundred years ago, and his music still lives in our hearts and minds — not because he wrote "classical" music, whatever that may mean, but because he provided us with an inexhaustible resource. A physical resource is depleted as we use it; an artistic one keeps offering more, the more we delve into it. This constitutes "greatness."

Applause Ignites the Actor's Spark

A FRIEND OF MINE, largely unacquainted with the entertainment business, expressed puzzlement and a little disgust at the insatiable need for applause that most performers display.

"So they get a poor audience once in a while," he said with a shrug. "It's not a big deal. At their salaries, they can afford to bomb occasionally."

His comment reminded me of a remark once made in an interview with Maurice Chevalier, the popular French performer. "I acquire my energy from my audience," he said.

It is a large part of the nature of actors that they draw their energy from their audiences, more than from their own internal dynamism. A responsive audience brings out the best in a performer, while an indifferent or apathetic one drains them of their essential vitality.

The performing arts are unlike the creative arts in this important respect. A painter, a writer, a composer uses solitude; an actor or comedian or musician "bounces off" public response. There is almost an electrical current that is turned on or off by a live audience.

The main reason that most actors and actresses prefer the

stage to the screen has less to do with "art" as such (though they may pretend it does) than with the fact that screen acting is done in little bits and chunks without an audience, and so the performer gets no "high" to carry him or her along from scene to scene.

Some of the most talented actors, like Alec Guiness, have openly expressed the feeling that they hardly exist as an independent personality when they are alone; it is only when they are involved in a role and interacting with an audience that they assume a real identity.

I suspect that one of the chief motives luring people into this line of work is a sense of emptiness in themselves, a kind of vacuum that can be satisfactorily filled only by making contact with a different appreciative public every night. Nobody else is so much at loose ends as an actor when he is not working at this chemical process.

Far more than most of us, the performer has a dreadful need to be liked and admired; this is the "energy" that Chevalier required and that vivifies everyone who goes on the stage. Just as a plain woman becomes more beautiful when she is loved, so an actor becomes more appealing when he excites applause for his impersonation.

True Artists Are Not Entertainers

SHORTLY BEFORE THE OPENING NIGHT of his magnificent opera *Don Giovanni,* Mozart remarked to a friend: "This opera is not calculated for the people of Vienna, it will be more justly appreciated at Prague; but, in reality, I have written it principally to please myself and my friends."

Whenever I am asked to distinguish between an "artist" and an "entertainer," this comment comes to mind. For Mozart, the supreme artist, was expressing the attitude held by every true artist in any field.

Of course, all creators would like their work to be appreciated. They care for fame, money, and honors as much as anyone else, although some pretend otherwise. But what marks them off from the mere entertainers is that their work must please themselves first and foremost.

A comedian will do almost anything to get a laugh from an audience, no matter how much beneath him it may be. An actor will mug horrendously to win a reaction, even though he (and the rest of the cast) is aware that he is pandering shamelessly to the groundlings. Writers of popular novels manipulate their readers without really respecting them.

It is not that the artist is "above" his audience — he is *beyond* it. By this I mean that he is looking further and deeper into the subtleties and complexities of his craft, and is in some way prophetic. He anticipates the future, rather than simply transcribing the past or present, even when he deals with traditional subjects.

"Pleasing" an audience means catering to its lowest common denominator; it is a kind of implied insult masquerading as a caress. The people who write sitcoms for television, on the whole, have contempt for the people who watch and enjoy them. They are mostly, perforce, failed artists who have turned themselves into entertainers.

It may be true, as Shaw said, that the first duty of an artist is to be interesting — but the question is: interesting to whom? Mozart's glorious music did not much interest fashionable audiences in Vienna, although he and a small coterie were aware that it was infinitely superior to the schmaltzy offerings in the salons. It was only in Prague, and not in his home city, that Mozart found a cordial reception.

The same distinction between the entertainer and the artist divides the politician from the statesman: The first tells the audience what it would like to hear, and wants to believe; the latter tells his hearers what they *ought* to know, despite their prejudices. Thus entertainers and politicians prosper, while artists and statesmen are more apt to languish, in their own time at least.

Shakespeare Meant to Be Heard, Not Seen

WATCHING LAURENCE OLIVIER'S PRODUCTION of *King Lear* on television reinforced my minority opinion that Shakespeare, on the whole, is better appreciated and understood now when he is read than when he is performed.

As a drama critic for more than thirty years, I have sat through dozens of Shakespearean productions, and I got little out of even the best of them, although I had the advantage of knowing the plots and characters almost as well as anyone.

It is my stubborn conviction that Shakespeare is written more to be *heard* than to be *seen;* and that the seeing does not intensify the hearing, but diminishes it. The period costumes, the scenery, the music (if any), the action itself detract from the great poetry. Many, if not most, of the glorious lines and passages are blurred and scanted by the visual distractions.

Olivier's *Lear* may have been a magnificent production, from a theatrical point of view; it was, like most, a disappointing experience from the poetical perspective. The director and the actors, as it were, got in the way of the play's inner power and expressiveness.

Shakespeare should "take place" in the mind, where it was conceived, and not on the stage — unless the stage is nearly bare, the actors are restrained, and the language is permitted to speak for itself without any ornamental activity.

If you think I am on the loony side for feeling this way, let me call to your attention Jane Donawerth's book *Shakespeare and the Sixteenth-Century Study of Language,* based on her doctoral dissertation, and published by the University of Illinois Press.

On the very first page of the text, Miss Donawerth informs

us that the Elizabethans felt much the same way I do: that they attended to "hear" a play more than to "see" one. Shakespeare himself wrote, "There is a lord will hear you play tonight," and his works were judged by contemporary audiences for their *language,* not for their absurdly improbable plots or their antic characters.

In the sonnets, where Shakespeare most reveals himself, he is ashamed and disgusted with his role as a playwright, considering it merely as a way to make a living by popular appeal, while holding only his poetry to be worthy of his talent. He thought so little of his plays as such that he never bothered to claim authorship for most of them, but he knew his sonnet sequence would be immortal.

No one should attend a Shakespeare play who has not first immersed himself in the text, and extracted all the meaning out of it — and once you do that, there is little need to see a realistic representation of the drama. For the reverence we pay to his name is like the reverence we exhibit in church, standing or kneeling for the rituals while we nod off during the sermon.

You Can't Think Thinking

SOME YEARS AGO, Wendell Johnson wrote a brilliant magazine article called "You Can't Write Writing." There is no such thing as "writing" in the abstract. You have to write about *something.* And that "something" is what determines the kind of writing you do. An essay, or a short story, or a research paper, or a political editorial — each calls for a different approach and a different set of linguistic and intellectual tools.

Almost nobody is an all-around "writer." I could not write a satisfactory short story if you put a gun to my head, although I have been a professional writer all my adult life. Many of the greatest novelists are nearly tongue-tied when it comes to writing an essay or a poem.

What is true for writing is equally true for thinking. You

cannot think thinking. You have to think about *something*. And what you think about, and the way you think about it, are shaped by your mind, your experiences, your passions and prejudices, your fears and expectations.

The "techniques of thinking," so widely advertised, cannot be taught, no matter what some educators or psychologists may believe. Thinking in the abstract is a futile and self-canceling process.

I remember that when I was an undergraduate, taking my first logic course, I became infatuated with the subject. "Wouldn't it be wonderful," I burbled to my logic professor, "if everybody were compelled to take a course in logic, and thus learn how to think rationally?"

But he was wiser than I was, and shook his head. "No," he replied, "logic must be taught as part of every course, not as an independent study. We learn how to think by dealing with specifics, not with forms or abstractions."

Obviously, if you begin with a false premise, the more logical your argument, the more certain it is that your conclusion will be false. What we need to learn and examine are our prior assumptions more than their logical implications.

Thinking cannot be divorced from feeling and wishing and hoping, and emotional affect generally. A whole person is involved in a subject of importance to him, not just a mind. Some of the world's greatest discoveries have been rejected by fine minds that were bound by logic and incapable of making an intuitive leap from their ingrained preconceptions.

There are no "thinking skills" as such. A man can think brilliantly on one subject, and come close to being an idiot on another. This is why "authority" does not, and should not, carry over from one field to another.

Nothing is so harmful to a reader as being made to believe he understands a subject that he does not understand.

Artist May Reveal Reality
Better Than Scientist

SPEAKING OF WORDS AND MEANINGS, as I was not long ago, re-minded me that in almost every case, when we use the word *real*, what we actually mean is "appearance." The way an object appears to us is real, and not the way it may be in itself.

What is a "realistic" painting of a table? It portrays the table as we see it — a solid and permanent entity, in wood or metal or plastic. But this is not the real table — the *Ding an sich,* as Kant called it. The object itself is a whirling mass of electrons; what we perceive as "substance" is a system of energy.

There is a famous story about Picasso engaged in painting the portrait of a woman, when her husband visited the studio. "What do you think of it?" the artist said. "Well," replied the husband, "it doesn't look much like her."

"Then how does she really look?" Picasso wanted to know. The husband drew a photograph from his wallet and said, "Like this." Picasso studied the photograph, and handed it back, saying, "Small, isn't she?"

It had never occurred to the husband that his wife was only two inches tall in the "realistic" photograph.

How would one paint a "realistic" picture of Medea, who killed her brother and slew her two infants; or of the mad emperor Nero; or of Alexander the Great, weeping that he had no more worlds to conquer? They all looked like ordinary people, but something inside them was distinctively different — and this internal element is what the artist tries to capture.

No appearance that we depict is realistic; all art is an abstraction from reality, for no two eyes see the same thing, or the thing-in-itself. Any dauber can paint sunflowers that look like sunflowers; it took a Van Gogh to make us see them in a new way, which is not botanical but metaphorical, or metaphysical, if you like.

All we can perceive is illusion of a sort; all we can know is how things seem to us, through our sensory apparatus. We cannot even see electrons, and yet they comprise the substructure of everything we call "matter."

"Time" and "space" are human categories, not natural ones. When an artist "distorts" these, he may be closer to the organic truth than the scientist has been yet able to approach. The visions of Blake may have more veracity than the telescopes of Galileo.

Poets Are Born, Not Made

THE ART OF WRITING, like the arts of painting or composing, cannot be "taught" in any formal or structured sense. It can be learned, which is a much different thing. It can be learned by reading a lot, and by writing a lot, but it requires an initial aptitude that is inborn.

A novice can learn to write better, or more accurately, more vividly, more thoughtfully, more persuasively — but only if the potential is already there, waiting to be elucidated by experience or repeated by trial-and-error.

Most classes in composition, and most teachers who offer courses in "writing," are as empty in their promise as those promoters who take splashy full-page ads telling people how they can make a fortune following the promoters' tips on business investments. Not one in a thousand will ever realize a profit on this, because moneymaking is a knack that cannot be imparted to others, and those possessing this talent don't need to be told how. It reminds me of the time a man brought his little son to Mozart for composing lessons, and was rejected.

"But, sir," the man protested, "you were composing at his age." "True," said Mozart, "but I didn't have to go to someone for lessons."

We seem to believe that everything that can be learned can be taught, which is a huge fallacy and misconception. Obviously, there are some disciplines, such as medicine or the law, which require formal training, no matter how much of a native flair one may have for them; but even here, it is the inherent "shape of mind" more than the course of study that separates the plodders from the paragons.

When Robert Hutchins was president of the University of Chicago, he used to say that college was for people who couldn't educate themselves (except, of course, for technical subjects), which meant most people. In the creative fields, certainly, the greatest achievers have been self-taught; and in some cases, academic training has crippled more than released creative powers.

We tend to place too much reliance on structured education, because that is the easiest way to put people into slots and keep them there. If Einstein hadn't published his papers on relativity, he might still be a patent clerk in Switzerland, for all the acknowledgment his genius could have brought him in official circles.

What is true of genius is equally true of lesser talents. Poets are born, as Horace said long ago, not made — although they can be made better and brought along by sympathetic criticism. But if they lack the crucial sense of self-criticism, no amount of "teaching" will help.

Nearly everyone with a typewriter imagines that he or she could be a "writer" with a little effort; nearly everyone with a camera supposes he or she could be a "photographer" with a little patience; but nobody is delusive enough to believe that simply being in possession of a piano or violin brings one any closer to being a "musician."

■

If we restrict the reading of certain books until minds are prepared for them, the minds will never be prepared for them.

Authors Mingle Fact with Fiction

How CLOSE to an actual living person can an author come in depicting a character in a novel? This is a problem that has confronted publishers, if not authors, for a long time, given the law of libel and the propensity to sue.

In a recent decision (which the lawyers like to call a "landmark case"), the New York Supreme Court dismissed a libel suit against a novelist who was accused by his former girlfriend of basing one of his fictional characters on her in a derogatory fashion.

It is difficult indeed to determine where liberty ends and license is taken in the novel. In one sense, every author draws upon the people he has known and met for characters in his book; the raw stuff of life is the very fabric of the imaginative work, and the author molds or remolds this into creative form.

On the other hand, no novelist of talent is a *realist* in the literal sense of the word. He takes attributes and traits from different persons and stitches them together; most characters in a novel are composites, with both their strengths and weaknesses emphasized for dramatic effect. He or she is cutting out dolls to resemble people, but the dolls are not people in the flesh.

A novel in which living personalities are limned is aptly called by the French a *roman à clef* — a story with a key. The key, of course, is knowing the identity of the real persons portrayed under different names in the novel. This, oddly enough, is almost the hardest kind of book to bring to life.

Perhaps the most famous, and brilliant, in this genre is Aldous Huxley's *Point Counter Point,* written in the late 1920s. The leading characters are witty and wicked representations of such famous figures of the day as D. H. Lawrence and his wife, Frieda, J. Middleton Murry and Katherine Mansfield, and Sir

Oswald Mosley, leader of the British fascist movement — not to mention Baudelaire in a modern transmutation.

(In possibly the greatest novel of our century, Proust's *Remembrance of Things Past,* the author did exactly the opposite: He disguised himself among his leading characters, concealing his Jewish background, his homosexuality, and his hypochondria by attributing them to his creations.)

Most aspiring authors whose novels are rejected complain bitterly that they were "true to life." But a photograph is not necessarily a work of art, and the art of the novelist is to commingle fact and fiction so skillfully that his world becomes more "real" than the world we see around us. In this sense, no authentic novel can libel a living person.

TV Is Modern Opium

A READER in Montana wanted to know how it is possible that television remains so bad when so many viewers complain about its low quality. "And not just intellectuals," he said, "but the kind of ordinary people I run into every day. Almost everyone is disgusted with television fare, and yet it seems to command a large, and even growing, audience."

I think that what we tend to forget in this appraisal is the basically *addictive* quality of television watching. The medium has assumed a social and psychological dimension in many people's lives that goes quite beyond its entertainment value or information content.

Because it captures the eye as well as the ear — while making relatively few demands on the mind — television serves as a surrogate for many relationships within the home and family. It provides an object of attention, as well as a way of narcotizing oneself against the reality of personal intercommunication.

It is a way to avoid conversation, to avert confronting others (or oneself), to shut out dissension, to lock oneself into an artificial environment. Reading, of course, used to supply some of this same effect — but most reading requires active participation of the mind, while TV viewing allows us to be passive, if not entirely comatose.

The general judgment seems to be that it is getting worse every year; even a highly paid performer like Johnny Carson regularly pokes fun at the "new" programs offered by the networks each season, all apparently trying to outstrip the others in asininity. No medium that so mocks itself can retain even a modicum of dignity or self-respect.

The addictive quality of TV resides in the function it performs, more than in the specific content of the programming — as the addiction to cigarettes is not so much in the nicotine as in the manual and oral satisfactions it provides in relieving tensions and anxieties imposed upon us by our jobs, families, or social obligations. (And just as the cigarette addict will prefer any weed he can grab to none at all, so the television addict will stupefyingly watch any program in preference to none, simply to close off participation in the real world. Obviously, there is nothing wrong in watching shows one genuinely enjoys, but so much viewing seems to be automatic, even compulsive.)

TV has become an "opium of the people" in a way Marx never envisioned in his famous epigram on religion, and its worldwide effect bids fair to become more universal than any religion has managed to be so far. With its limitless potential for good, TV poignantly illustrates once more the truth of the old Roman adage that "the worst is a corruption of the best."

Television violence does not so much stimulate *violence in the real world as, by making violence seem a familiar everyday event, it inures the public to acts of brutality and creates a callousness that ends in passive acceptance of such misdeeds as an inevitable part of life.*

Classical Music Is Best Under the Stars

IT SEEMS TO ME that a great deal of the apathy, if not downright antagonism, toward what is known as "classical" music comes from its formal setting and structure as much as from its musical form.

Looking back on my experiences of listening to chamber music, for instance, the performances that remain most vivid in my mind are those that harmonized with a natural setting and blended with the landscape, not where we sat on stiff chairs in military rows in starched attire. I think of the concerts under the tent in Aspen (Colorado), in the lounge at "Wildacres" (North Carolina), within the handcrafted barn beams at Birch Creek (Wisconsin). Not to mention the spacious *piazza* in Rappallo and other outdoor sites throughout Italian towns.

So-called serious music was not meant to be taken somberly or pompously, with hushed reverence, as a cultural event, even though the most exuberant compositions are often played that way. People tend to put on their "classical" faces at a concert, just as they put on their "religious" faces at a church service.

But both religion and music are meaningless if they are separated from the mainstream of life. Bach, Beethoven, Mozart, all the great composers, were vividly aware of this — their music is meant to penetrate to the core of our humanity, not to float above in some ethereal realm reserved for special occasions.

What we call "art," in the broadest sense, is not the exclusive domain of a few exalted souls but a part of the very warp and woof of human culture, from the most primitive to the most sophisticated. It is not meant to be something that divides, but something that unites.

It is the formal social structuring in most concerts that tends to erect artificial barriers between the classical and the popular fields. Actually, there are only two kinds of music: good and bad, and just as much junk is played in the concert halls as is ever heard in more plebeian settings.

Serious music, in a class society even like ours, soon becomes the captive of the more privileged class, for reasons that usually have nothing to do with its intrinsic excellence, but because it is viewed as one of the appurtenances of privilege. (Veblen long ago shrewdly anatomized this link between high culture and high income.)

It is not enjoyed in the "land of high culture and high income" as much as it is endured. Where it is most enjoyed is under the stars, in a tent, in a mountain lodge, in a lofty barn, or in a plaza dotted with tables and umbrellas and carafes of wine.

White ties and tails may be appropriate for a coronation; they are absurd anachronisms when they are worn by a conductor and performers, for they turn a musical celebration into a social ritual that only distances the performance from the audience and turns the composer into a frozen figurehead of "culture."

Why Is Modern Art More Popular Than Modern Music?

OFTEN WHEN A COMMENTATOR says he is puzzled about a certain subject, he is being falsely modest and is just getting the reader to think along with him while he obliquely expounds his own point of view.

But I am genuinely puzzled about something that I wish my more artistically sophisticated readers could enlighten me about. And that is the difference in acceptance and status between modern music and modern painting.

Modern music is hardly played at all in the concert halls. The orchestral societies say this is because nobody wants to attend these concerts. Audiences want to hear the music they are used to, which means the old classic and romantic composers before the twentieth century.

In the field of modern art, I cannot believe that most people are infatuated with the abstract expressionists, or prefer them to Rembrandt and Monet. Yet the canvases of painters like Kandinsky and Jackson Pollock command millions, and every art museum pants for an exhibit of their works.

A comparable composer, working in the modern vein, is lucky if one of his pieces is publicly performed once a year. Even the members of the orchestra aren't crazy about rehearsing and playing his music.

Yet there is no reason to believe that the field of serious music doesn't produce at least the same proportion of first-rate talents that the field of painting does. Statistically, there should be a half dozen or more contemporary composers who are sought after as fervently as the top painters.

Does a canvas command a million dollars because it is a material object as well as a piece of art, while music cannot be bought and hung on a wall and traded as a physical commodity? Obviously, an original score signed by a composer has little value compared with an original canvas — even if it were signed by a Mozart or a Beethoven.

Is it that musical audiences are simply duller or dumber or more conventional than the audiences for painting? Or are the newer composers really far inferior to the modern painters? Whatever the reason, it does seem a pity that a serious composer has to teach or marry into money in order to pursue the Muse.

Music is so integral a part of our culture that it is hard to understand how the late Richard Rodgers, a Broadway melodist, could have earned $100 million from his music, while at the same time a Bartók died in a hospital, sustained in his last days only by the charity of a conductor friend. Or why

Rodgers felt it necessary to expiate his popular success by endowing a foundation for giving scholarships to serious composers.

Translations Fail to Capture Nuance

THERE IS an old Italian saying in scholarly circles, *"Traduttore traditore,"* which means "a translator is a traitor" and implies that it is impossible to translate without misrepresenting the original.

I thought of this when I read Bruno Bettelheim's fascinating article on "Freud and the Soul" in *The New Yorker* magazine. His complaint was that poor English translations of Freud do not accurately reflect the humanism he desired at the heart of psychoanalysis. In reading it, I also recalled the words the French philosopher Jacques Maritain expressed at Aspen some years ago. He was dissatisfied with all his many books translated into English because "the translators who knew French did not know philosophy, and those who knew philosophy did not know French."

The fact is that, while there are better and worse translations, even someone who knew both French and philosophy might have difficulty in converting French to English and vice versa — because there is no one-to-one correlation between many words and phrases in these two languages. (This, by the way, is why all languages have borrowed words from other tongues, and why scores of English words are heard in all European and Asiatic languages.)

As an example, French does not have a word precisely corresponding to our *chair*. A Frenchman can say *"chaise"* or *"fauteuil,"* depending on the context, but there is no generic "chair," as in English. German has no word for an animal kept as a pet; the German word for "domestic animal" certainly doesn't fill the bill. And we, having no word for older people, like the French *viellard,* had to invent the awful "senior citizen."

Literal translations are the worst. Mario Pei tells us that during World War II the Italians got one of their few laughs out of the literal translation of the British "Home Fleet" (*"Flotta di Casa"*), which to them sounded like a domesticated tomcat. And when Fats Waller's song "Ain't Misbehavin' " was beamed to Russian radio, it was rendered as "I Don't Do Anything Bad," which misses the whole flavor of it.

Freud no doubt has been wretchedly mistranslated (and thus misunderstood), but probably no worse than anyone else whose ideas are novel, complex, or subtle. Actually, even within the same language, a different use of the same word can impede or paralyze communication.

An important conference, not long ago, between British and American officials ground to a halt when the British asked to "table" a resolution and the Americans objected. It turned out, however, that *to table* in Britain is to put it on the table for consideration, whereas in America it means to put it aside. So what chance did Freud have?

The reason that truth is stranger than fiction is that fiction has to have a rational thread running through it in order to be believable, whereas reality may be totally irrational.

■

Those who complain that book reviewers pay too much attention to "serious" books and not enough to popular ones fail to understand that the proper function of a critic is to call attention to worthwhile books that might otherwise be neglected, and not to confirm the popular taste, which needs no stimulation.

Honesty Is the Best Propaganda

THE OLD MAXIM that "Honesty is the best policy" may be rejected by the cynical, but I think a more convincing case can be made out for the fact that "Honesty is the best propaganda" for almost every cause.

What directly prompts this reflection is my weekly addiction to the television program *Hill Street Blues,* which is the only show on commercial channels that I never miss if I can possibly help it. It is, to my mind, the best written, best acted, and best directed offering in the entire medium.

Even more important than its entertainment value, however, is its most persuasive ability to provide the average viewer with a sympathetic portrait of a police precinct in urban slums. One of my friends, an inveterate cop-hater, remarked the other night that this show alone had, for the first time, changed her feelings about the police force. It changed them, not by showing police heroics or by pretending that these men are better than anyone else, but simply by presenting them as fallible human beings caught in difficult circumstances and having to make hard, realistic decisions that are sometimes right and sometimes wrong.

It is not propaganda for "law and order" or any of the other familiar clichés of police stories. Its personnel are as varied as any other group of people — including the weak, the bigoted, and the venal, as well as the straight and the courageous. This is precisely what makes it so effective as propaganda — because it is not aimed at that end, but at the end of showing how diverse human beings react to difficult and dangerous situations, without bravado or derring-do, or the foolish antics of most cops-and-robbers depictions.

The viewer gets to know, and identify with, these police men and women with all their foibles and frailties, their temptations and ambitions, in a far more realistic way than any soap opera would dare. And the net effect is to enlist our sympathies more strongly than any overt propaganda could ever achieve by a direct assault on our emotions.

Hill Street Blues is most of all credible, because it gives us the substance and not merely the symbol of police work and is willing to show the warts and imperfections of both the people and the system, in order to provide a well-rounded portrait of urban tensions and conflict.

Propaganda has turned into an ugly word these days, although it was not so originally — and would not have become so if those who propagated their viewpoints were as honest as they were zealous.

Thinking It Through Before Writing It Down

WHEN THE GREAT FRENCH DRAMATIST RACINE had mapped out the scenes of a play, he would announce to friends, "My tragedy is finished" — though he had not written a line of the actual dialogue.

What the average person fails to recognize about most creative work is that it is not only generated in the mind but is also completed there, long before it may be put to paper or canvas. And this process is as true in the field of scientific formulas as it is in writing or painting or musical composition. The real work is done in the head; the rest is only manual or physical transposition of the idea into tangible form.

The mathematical genius Karl Friedrich Gauss once remarked, "I have been sure of my results for some time; what I don't know is how I shall arrive at them."

Both the artist and the scientist think symbolically, not literally. The practical aspect of their work is relatively simple: putting down marks on a piece of paper. It is the conceptual part that is hard and may take months or years to germinate; what is loosely called "inspiration" is only the tail end of a sustained (and often unconscious) process.

In his book *Greatness in Music,* Alfred Einstein, an eminent musicologist and critic, observed that Mozart composed with such seeming rapidity because he was simply transcribing what had already taken final form in his mind, much as a stenographer merely copies from shorthand notes or a manuscript.

Within my own smaller compass, it is equally true that by the time I sit down to write a column, I already know what I am going to say — in a real sense, it has already been composed — and the physical act of putting it to paper is only a technical matter of no great moment. What is commonly judged to be good writing is 90 percent clear thinking — not necessarily correct thinking, but coherent and unified.

It is popularly believed that Lincoln scratched out his famous "Gettysburg Address" on the back of an old envelope en route to the ceremony, and this may very well be true. But who can doubt that the philosophical notion embodied in that memorable dedication had been "cooking," as it were, in the oven of his unconscious for many a moon?

If a creative work — be it a poem, a painting, a melody, or a theorem — does not in some sense come easily, we may be sure it is not ready yet to leave the oven, which may be why we term such offerings *half-baked.* In the realms of art or science, ripeness is all.

I have never agreed that one picture is worth a thousand words, but it is certainly true that one slogan can blot out a thousand thoughts.

■

Why do so many children's books have large print, when youngsters see so well, and adult books have small print for adults who don't?

Audience Must Meet Artist Halfway

WHEN OSCAR WILDE was asked how one of his new plays was faring on the London stage, he replied airily, "The play is a great success — but the audience is a failure." As usual with Wilde, his retort was part arrogance and part truth.

We accept the fact that it takes two to tango, and it takes two to make a quarrel, and it takes two to make a marriage work — but when it comes to the arts, we suppose it takes only one, and that one is the artist.

"To have great poets," Walt Whitman said a century ago, "we must have great audiences, too." He meant that all art is a collaborative enterprise between the creator and the audience, and each bears a share of the responsibility for the success or failure of the work.

In modern society, more than ever before, we have come to expect the artist to do all the work for us. We look upon a play or a painting or a piece of music as a commodity designed expressly to satisfy us in the same way as a handbag, a hamburger, or a highball.

But the best artists, throughout history, have made *demands* upon us. They ask that we actively participate in the work, not that we be passive spectators or mere consumers of their products. What they give us is not a commodity but a projection of their imagination — and what we do with it is as important as the way they present it.

Obviously, if the artist is too far removed from his audience, little contact will be made. He has an obligation to offer his work in a way that is decipherable to his age and his culture. James Joyce was a salutary influence for other writers, as a bold experimenter in form, but a dead end for the general reader.

When Stravinsky first began composing, or Picasso began experimenting with new forms of painting, they were regarded as cockeyed or perverse by conventional audiences; but their art was so powerful that, before long, what had seemed like dissonances in music and distortions in painting came to be appreciated as new ways of hearing and seeing.

It has long seemed strange to me that the public is avid for "newness" in its material wants and needs but bitterly resists whatever is new in the imaginative world. As we know, the incomparable Beethoven was attacked by the critics of his day for "violating" some of the most sacred canons of musical composition; but in less than a century, he turned into a "classic."

Art is not there primarily to make us feel good, to stuff us, or to cater to our sense of the familiar or comfortable. Its main function is to prompt us out of our intellectual and emotional ruts and get us to share in the artist's vision. We have a right, of course, to reject his vision; but we first have an obligation to rise to meet it, to make sure that the "failure" is in the work of art, and not in our conventional response to it.

Less Is More

MIES VAN DER ROHE is famous not only for his modern architecture but for his maxim that "Less is more." If this is true for the design of a building, it also holds true in respect to other arts and crafts.

A while ago I was listening to Marilyn Horne giving a telecast concert from Lincoln Center. The program consisted largely of folksongs, from "Danny Boy" and "Shenandoah" to the down-home melodies of Stephen Foster. I must confess that, lovely as her voice is, I turned away from the progam. It was not that she failed to do justice to the songs; it was that she did them more than justice — her superbly trained voice overpowered both the music and the lyrics.

Opera singers, on the whole, can no more perform popular music than classical instrumentalists can render jazz. In one sense, technically, they are too good for it; in another sense, emotionally, they are not good enough. Popular music calls for special talents that not only are not required, but are positively shunned, in classical training.

Less is more in such performances, and more is less. The very artistry that is sought in operas and recitals acts as a barrier to the cadences and syncopations of jazz and blues and even gospel music.

I have heard dozens of magnificent opera stars, of both sexes, essay popular tunes, and always with disappointing results; and it is the same with instrumentalists. Many years ago, I visited a nightclub with a distinguished violinist and conductor, to hear Eddie South, the "Dark Angel" of the violin — and the maestro freely admitted that he would be incapable of fiddling this music to life as vividly as the jazz artist.

Ballet dancers, to cite a similar case, make notoriously bad partners for ballroom dancing. All their formal training is against it, even when they are exponents of the "modern" dance à la Martha Graham. There is a whole different kinetic world involved, just as there is between the sustained note of an aria and the "slide" of a crooner or a street singer.

Actually, the distinction we habitually make between "classical" and "popular" music is a false and snobbish one. The only two kinds of music are "good" and "bad," and there is just as much bad classical music per score as bad popular music. Personally, I prefer to hear what is called good "bad" music to bad "good" music, if forced to make that choice.

And I would certainly rather listen to Judy Collins doing "Jeannie with the Light Brown Hair" than Marilyn Horne struggling to temper her voice to the naïve limitations of a folksong. When less is more, more can be far too much to take.

Sophistication may not get you into trouble as often as naïveté can, but the trouble it can get you into is worse and lasts longer than the naïve ever have to endure.

Today's Youth Crave Music

IF ANY SINGLE WORD were to characterize the rising generation, I would suggest it is *music*. For, more than at any other time in living memory, the melodies and lyrics of modern music seem to encapsulate and to animate young people and even those well into their thirties.

You may not care to call it music, if you find the rhythms repulsive and the lyrics banal, but however it is designated, the new music is undoubtedly a prime element in the emotional lives of the young. Far more so than in my generation or any previous one recorded in history.

Part of the popularity may be attributed to the prevalence and fidelity of acoustical equipment. Yet this alone would not account for the powerful, almost addictive, hold that records and tapes and cassettes exert upon nearly everyone under forty — not only in the United States but throughout the developed world.

In my time, and before, music was important for dancing or romancing or background gaiety at parties. Today it is more like a way of life, a statement, or a stimulant or a narcotic; it serves a broad spectrum of purposes and needs that goes far beyond anything in the past.

Nor has it affected only those with undeveloped tastes. My older daughter would walk six miles through a snowstorm to hear an all-Bach concert — yet she, too, is a captive of modern music, and cannot ease herself behind the wheel of a car before she has turned on the radio or the tape deck, no matter how deplorable the program.

I cannot begin to explain this absorption in music, having grown up in a different environment, where music played an important, but subordinate, role in my emotional and social life. I did not feel acutely deprived by silence, as young people do now, who cannot study or read without music.

It is more than a fad, I am convinced, more than a passing infatuation with a highly accessible form of entertainment. There is some deeper psychological craving that this music caters to, some appetite that can hardly be satiated in any other way. "Addictive" is hardly too strong to describe it.

Youth is stirring uneasily throughout the world. For the first time, perhaps, it feels a greater kinship with members of its own generation, wherever they may live, than with their own compatriots of an older age. Music is breaking down nationalistic barriers faster than they can be erected or repaired by self-seeking governments; and the legendary "universality" of music — hitherto more myth than reality — may be finally coming into its own.

We cannot understand the period we are living in, any more than a fish can comprehend the water it swims in. I suggest that the social scientists start paying more attention to the phenomenon of music in contemporary life; it may offer them more insights into the probable future than the ponderous academic research perpetrated by people who are, culturally at least, tone-deaf.

Art Is Emotion Recollected in Tranquillity

THE MOST EFFECTIVE WRITING is put down on paper in a cool mood, not a heated one — no matter how heated the prose may seem to be when it is publicly read. Creativity of any kind is a calculated act, not a burst of feeling. This is something that people outside the arts find hard to grasp — and that many novice writers or musicians or actors find equally hard to learn. But the fact is that the more strongly you feel something, the worse you express it at that particular moment.

The actor who seems to be "living" his part on the stage is one who has achieved artistic distance from the role and is able to interpret it so that he seems to be totally involved; but if he really were, he could not give that impression.

An actor "gets into" his part when he is rehearsing it; it is then that he identifies with the emotions and reactions of the character and puts on a second skin, as it were; but if he identifies emotionally when the curtain goes up, his performance inevitably suffers.

Much the same is true in the performance of music. A concert pianist must be more than a mere player of notes, must saturate herself in the mood and feeling of the composer when learning the piece.

Whenever I feel impassioned about a subject and sit down to write it in a red-hot frame of mind, the result is overstrained and overwritten and thus is less persuasive than when I have cooled down and allowed myself some distance from my own feelings.

Indeed, in the writing craft, there is no relation between the way one feels at the time and the nature of the work that is turned out. Countless writers have testified that they penned their most amusing pieces while in the slough of despond and some of their bleakest when they were riding the crest of good spirits.

The arts, indeed, are as much *re-creation* as creation. The practitioner re-creates what he has felt in the past, what he has captured in his permanent unconscious, and brings it to life when it is ready to be born, and not on the basis of his daily feelings. Otherwise, Mozart or Schubert would have composed hardly anything but tragic music.

There is nothing "natural" about the arts, for nature is spontaneous and randomized, while the arts are structured and focused as symbols for our feelings, not as the feelings themselves. The arts are imitations of life, containing truths that nature is incapable of expressing, truths that we are capable of expressing only after the fact, not during the experience.

It seems an odd contradiction that the people who have the best table manners generally serve the worst food.

■

Americans traveling abroad who seek out the company of other Americans have found the surest way of learning the least about foreign cultures.

■

A "humanist" is a man who has been typing manuscripts all his life and still can't change a ribbon.

■

Dishonest men who operate outside the law are sent to prison; dishonest men who manipulate the law are given testimonial banquets.

■

What most advertisers can't seem to grasp is that people are more likely to believe something that is whispered to them than something that is shouted at them.

■

Nothing is more uncomfortable than being praised by someone whose opinion you hold in low esteem.

■

A private club is not designed so much to take people in as to keep people out; the status of a club is recognized more by the latter than by the former.

■

Money is the one object that violates the laws of perspective: it always looks larger far away from you than it does when in your hands.

It is hardly surprising that so many former radicals have become "neo-conservatives" with the passing years — those personalities who are attracted to one extreme in their youth are temperamentally attracted to its opposite as they grow older.

■

It may be perfectly true that "boys will be boys," but why do men have to remain boys so much longer than women remain girls?

■

One sure way to detect a crank is that he always advances a single determining cause for the fall and decline of Rome, instead of adducing a subtle combination of forces operating at the same time.

■

It is impossible to have faith without a deep reservoir of patience, which is why quick minds tend to be skeptical.

■

In a rational society, such popular works of entertainment as novels, musicals, and so on, which earn beyond a certain amount, would be assessed a percentage of profits, the funds going to support the serious arts, in museums, dramatic groups, and other non-profit ventures.

■

In 1800, the per capita income in developed countries was three times that of underdeveloped countries; in 1914, it was seven times greater; currently, the citizen of a developed nation has twelve times the income of a person in an underdeveloped one — and we expect to halt the spread of revolutions by rhetoric about "freedom."

A man should dress as though he cares how he looks, but not as though he cares how other people think he looks.

■

If nature was really interested in our welfare, it would have made health catching instead of disease.

■

"Believers" tend to believe in God's vengeance for their enemies, but in God's mercy for themselves.

■

Whenever I hear the phrase "human nature" I wince, because it is certain that the speaker is going to stress a part of it at the expense of the whole of it.

■

If the Devil finds work for idle hands, as our mothers used to warn us, how much more mischief do you suppose he finds for idle minds?

■

Nobody cares to hear your troubles, unless they are troubles he or she has also experienced; misery may love company, but company tolerates only the kinds of misery it has already known.

■

If our globe experiences a massive nuclear conflict, those who manage to survive it will assure the rest that only "deterrence" prevented it for so long. (Some sweet consolation!)

■

I have never believed any historical panorama purporting to show us "The Dawn of Civilization" because it seems plain to me that dawn hasn't broken yet.

It's a popular anachronism to call a man "a gentleman and a scholar" in our society, which secretly regards the gentleman as a weakling and the scholar as a misfit.

■

Real frustration is not the difference between what we have and what we would like to have, but the difference between what we are and what we would like to be.

■

If you removed movie stars and athletes from consideration, most Americans could not fill a list of the ten people in the world they most admire.

■

A womanizer is a man who finds pursuit of a woman irresistible, and possession of her intolerable.

■

We are generally so vain and inconsistent that we even resent the fact that we weren't invited to a party we didn't want to attend.

■

The Vandals of history invaded a region and destroyed property; the modern Vandals develop property and destroy a region. (Which is worse?)

■

Other people's faults may amuse or exasperate us; but it is when we glimpse our own faults displayed or exaggerated in another that we really get upset.

■

"God helps those who help themselves," murmured the thief as he broke a window and helped himself to a TV set.